CW00487121

THE LANGUAGES OF ARC

Social Archaeology

General Editor: Ian Hodder, Stanford University

Advisory Editors
Margaret Conkey, University of California at Berkeley
Mark Leone, University of Maryland
Alain Schnapp, UER d'Art et d'Archéologie, Paris
Stephen Shennan, University of Southampton
Bruce Trigger, McGill University, Montreal

Titles in Print

ARCHAEOLOGIES OF LANDSCAPE
Edited by Wendy Ashmore and A. Bernard Knapp

TECHNOLOGY AND SOCIAL AGENCY
Marcia-Anne Dobres

ENGENDERING ARCHAEOLOGY
Edited by Joan M. Gero and Margaret W. Conkey

SOCIAL BEING AND TIME
Christopher Gosden

THE ARCHAEOLOGY OF ISLAM
Timothy Insoll

AN ARCHAEOLOGY OF CAPITALISM
Matthew Johnson

THE LANGUAGES OF ARCHAEOLOGY
Rosemary A. Joyce with Robert W. Preucel, Jeanne Lopiparo, Carolyn Guyer, and Michael Joyce

ARCHAEOLOGIES OF SOCIAL LIFE
Lynn Meskell

ARCHAEOLOGY AS CULTURAL HISTORY
Ian Morris

CONTEMPORARY ARCHAEOLOGY IN THEORY
Robert W. Preucel and Ian Hodder

BEREAVEMENT AND COMMEMORATION
Sarah Tarlow

METAPHOR AND MATERIAL CULTURE
Christopher W. Tilley

In preparation

THE RISE OF MESO-AMERICA
Elizabeth Brumfiel

COMPANION TO SOCIAL ARCHAEOLOGY
Lynn Meskell and Robert W. Preucel

ARCHAEOLOGICAL SEMIOTICS
Robert W. Preucel

The Languages of Archaeology

Dialogue, Narrative, and Writing

Rosemary A. Joyce

with *Robert W. Preucel, Jeanne Lopiparo,*
Carolyn Guyer, and *Michael Joyce*

Blackwell
Publishers

Chapters 1, 3, 6, and 7 © Rosemary A. Joyce 2002.
Chapter 2 © Rosemary A. Joyce and Robert W. Preucel 2002.
Chapter 4 © Jeanne Lopiparo 2002.
Chapter 5 © Rosemary A. Joyce, Carolyn Guyer and Michael Joyce 2002.

Editorial Offices:
108 Cowley Road, Oxford OX4 1JF, UK
  Tel: +44 (0)1865 791100
350 Main Street, Malden, MA 02148-5018, USA
  Tel: +1 781 388 8250

The right of Rosemary A. Joyce to be identified as the author of chapters 1, 3, 6, 7, and co-author of chapters 2 and 5 of this work has been asserted in accordance with the UK Copyright, Designs and Patents Act 1988.

The right of Robert W. Preucel to be identified as the co-author of chapter 2 of this work has been asserted in accordance with the UK Copyright, Designs and Patents Act 1988.

The right of Jeanne Lopiparo to be identified as the author of chapter 4 of this work has been asserted in accordance with the UK Copyright, Designs and Patents Act 1988.

The right of Carolyn Guyer and Michael Joyce to be identified as the co-authors of chapter 5 of this work has been asserted in accordance with the UK Copyright, Designs and Patents Act 1988.

All rights reserved. No part of this publication may be reproduced, stored in a retrieval system, or transmitted, in any form or by any means, electronic, mechanical, photocopying, recording or otherwise, except as permitted by the UK Copyright, Designs and Patents Act 1988, without the prior permission of the publisher.

First published 2002 by Blackwell Publishers Ltd, a Blackwell Publishing company

Library of Congress Cataloging-in-Publication Data

Joyce, Rosemary A., 1956–
    The languages of archaeology : dialogue, narrative, and writing / Rosemary A. Joyce, with Robert W. Preucel, Jeanne Lopiparo, Carolyn Guyer, and Michael Joyce.
        p. cm. – (The languages of archaeology)
    ISBN 0-631-22178-6 (hbk) ISBN 0-631-22179-4 (pbk)
    1. Archaeology – Methodology. 2. Rhetoric. 3. Technical writing.
4. Narration (Rhetoric) 5. Discourse analysis. I. Preucel, Robert W.
II. Lopiparo, Jeanne. III. Guyer, Carolyn. IV. Title. V. Series.
    CC75.7 .J69 2002
    930.1 – dc21   2002001347

A catalogue record for this title is available from the British Library.

Set in Garamond
by SNP Best-set Typesetter Ltd., Hong Kong
Printed and bound in Great Britain by TJ International, Padstow, Cornwall

For further information on
Blackwell Publishers, visit our website:
www.blackwellpublisher.co.uk

Contents

Figures

Acknowledgments

Parts of chapters 1 and 5 were originally written and presented at the conference "Doing Archaeology as a Feminist" at the School of American Research (April, 1998), organized by Alison Wylie and Meg Conkey. A revised version of the portions of that paper incorporated here was presented at the annual meeting of the Society for American Archaeology (Chicago, 1999), in a session organized by Kevin Bartoy. Rosemary Joyce would like to thank these organizers, the other participants at the SAR conference, and members of the audience at SAA who offered specific comments on these presentations. She is especially indebted to Julia Hendon, Carol McDavid, Lynn Meskell, Stephanie Moser, and Alison Wylie for their encouragement of her engagement with issues raised in these papers.

The original version of the first dialogue, in chapter 2, was written for and presented in the session "Doing Archaeology As if it Mattered" at the 93rd Annual Meeting of the American Anthropological Association (Atlanta, 1994), organized by Meg Conkey and Ruth Tringham. Rosemary Joyce would like thank Bob Preucel for extending the invitation to collaborate on this paper. Preucel and Joyce thank the organizers for the invitation to participate and Alison Wylie, discussant for the session, for her comments. They also gratefully acknowledge the collaboration of Meredith Chesson and Erika Evasdottir on the survey of textbooks cited in this dialogue. Leslie Atik provided the alternative metaphor of fieldwork-as-cultivation, for which we are indebted to her.

Joyce's analysis of burials from Tlatilco, Mexico, in chapter 6 was originally presented in the Dumbarton Oaks Pre-Columbian Symposium "Social Patterns in Pre-Classic Mesoamerica" (1993). She would like to thank David C. Grove for the opportunity to co-organize and participate in this conference, and Elizabeth Boone, then Director of Pre-Columbian Studies, for her encouragement. The first version of the reanalysis of these burials incorporated in chapter 7 was presented at the Third Archaeology and Gender Conference held at Appalachian State University in Boone, North Carolina in 1994, organized by Cheryl Claassen. A reworked version was presented at the annual meeting of the American Anthropological Association in 1997, in the session "New Perspectives on Mortuary Ritual" organized by Meredith Chesson and Ian Kuijt. Joyce thanks the organizers of both conferences, and the discussants of the AAA session, Susan Kus, Ken George, and Tom Dillehay, for their comments. Part of the introductory discussion in chapter 6 is based on material first published in "Women's Work: Images of Production and Reproduction in Prehispanic Southern Central America", by Rosemary A. Joyce, which appeared in *Current Anthropology* 34: 255–74 (1993).

Finally, the risks taken by the many experimental writers whose works are discussed here should be acknowledged; without them, there would be no material for this book. In the pages that follow, I attempt to treat their work seriously, meaning that I question what the unintended effects of those works are, as well as seeking to understand the intentional goals of the writers. While, as a participant in experimental writing, self-reflection is one of my own goals, I can predict that I am less aware of my own production of unintended, and potentially problematic, effects. The advantage of critically considering the work of scholars whose attempts to innovate I admire is that I can see more clearly what they have accomplished. I hope the authors of these works will appreciate the sincerity of my regard for their work, and I urge every reader of this book to see for themselves what innovative archaeological writers discussed herein have done. Disagreement is only contradiction unless there are two different subjects to make it into a dialogue (Bakhtin 1984: 183). "We only come to know what we have written by understanding the choices of others ... We understand from the third person what we have written in the first person, but only in the process of reading the second person" (M. Joyce 1995: 237).

R.A.J.
November 2001

The authors and publishers would like to thank the following for permission to reproduce copyright material: photographs of Maya pottery, copyright Justin Kerr, were used with permission as sources for images in *Crafting Cosmos* featured in chapter 4.

Introduction

This book examines the nature of archaeological writing. In it, I employ concepts from literary theory to examine practices through which archaeologists create representations of the past while simultaneously reproducing the discipline itself. I argue that a process of creating narratives permeates archaeology from the initial moments of investigation of sites through to the production of texts, a term which should be understood to include far more than written materials like this book. My emphasis is less on the specific structures employed in such archaeological narratives than on the event of narrativization, an event which is, I suggest, always an act of social communication. To understand archaeological storytelling implies not only understanding how archaeologists come to the knowledge they hold, but also how archaeological knowledge creates different communities. Telling stories speaks to and connects diverse circles of participants engaged in attempts to understand the past.

In 1989, Ian Hodder published a brief article, "Writing archaeology," which raised the basic issues this book will address (Hodder 1989b). Contrasting a late eighteenth-century archaeological field report with its late-twentieth-century descendants, he called for archaeologists to reflect on their writing practices, as ethnographers and historians were then already doing. He specifically identified rhetoric, narrative, and dialogue as crucial topics for archaeological reflection. These concepts are central to this book.

Ten years later, there has been an explosion of experimentation with new forms of writing within archaeology, fueled by sources including feminism, post-structuralism, and critiques of representation from descendant groups who see archaeological sites as their cultural heritage. Yet this vibrant experimentation *with* writing has yet to include a sustained critical examination *of* writing. This book explores the nature of narrative and the significance of dialogue within archaeological writing. It incorporates writing experiments and a sustained critique of both conventional and experimental archaeological writing. Through the examination of a selection of different kinds of archaeological texts, this book demonstrates how the creation of narratives is a practice that literally binds the discipline of archaeology together from the field through to formal and informal presentation of interpretations.

While presented as a study of archaeological *writing*, one of the central goals of this book is to demonstrate that narrative, in a broad sense, is constitutive of archaeology. The writing of archaeology begins long before an author puts pen to page. The narratives that archaeologists begin to construct in the field, lab, and classroom enter formal texts as echoed voices. These narratives are themselves engagements with already voiced dialogues from our disciplinary history and discourse about the past from outside the discipline. Telling ourselves stories as we engage in primary research, we construct already narrativized knowledge, which then appears more natural in its transcription in written texts. Archaeological texts themselves, of course, consist of more than linear transcriptions of words. The naturalization of these texts draws on a variety of nonlinguistic discursive practices, such as the incorporation of particular kinds of figures and the deployment of tables of statistics. These graphic elements work with and against the verbal texts with which they are conjoined to produce an aura of factuality about archaeological interpretation. The complex intertextuality that contributes to the construction of archaeological texts, in all its dimensions, is the subject of this study.

This book thus offers a *general* critique of archaeology as a discipline engaging in the present in the construction of persuasive stories about imagined pasts. For this discussion to be sufficiently complex, it must also consider the relations created between the narrators and auditors of archaeological narratives. Stories are interpreted by audiences whose diversity is rarely fully anticipated by the archaeologist-narrators, who increasingly find themselves engaged in dialogues beyond disciplinary boundaries. The chapters that follow argue that all archaeological discourse, regardless of its format and audience, is dialogic. The formation of marked genres – including site reports and more popular media, such as museum exhibits – are formalizations of specific dialogues, amenable to analysis as genres. Archaeology is a textual practice from the field through the lab and into all forms of dissemination. By taking the narratives of archaeology as including the formalization of stories in the field and lab, this book demonstrates how the writing practices of archaeology serve to discipline very different forms of text production that take place *before* the creation of authoritative written narratives. Employing Mikhail Bakhtin's theoretical vocabulary and concepts from Roland Barthes's discussions of narrative, the chapters that follow examine how traces of the original narratives of field and lab continue to inhabit written texts as multiple voices that produce an inherent dialogism of the kind Bakhtin discusses in his works. The dialogic nature of archaeology is a strength that should be highlighted even more than it has been in the experimental writing of recent years.

Concern with the nature of writing (in the narrow sense) is of long standing in related human sciences. In history, Hayden White (1973, 1978, 1987) is credited with analyzing the way that the *forms* of historical writing were themselves part of the histories they created. In North American social anthropology, the examination of writing given prominence by postmodernist ethnographers (Clifford and Marcus 1986, Marcus and Fischer 1986), and further developed by contemporary feminist ethnographers (Behar and Gordon 1995, Wolf 1992) who follow a long-established tradition of experimental writing by feminist anthropologists (Visweswaran 1994, 1997), has involved substantial consideration of the relations between the represented subject and the author shaping that subject through writing. But despite occasional citations of these and related discussions, archaeology at present lacks a single integrated discussion of these topics. In the pages that follow, the contributors to this project attempt to begin that discussion.

Faithful to Bakhtin's admonition to seek to achieve dialogue in life and art both, this book is constructed as a collaboration between a number of writers. The different voices are introduced in the chapters that follow as specifically situated in the work of understanding archaeological meaning. The relations between the voices, which become clear through these dialogues, include those of specialists and nonspecialists, professors and students, masters and apprentices in the fieldwork of archaeology, present inheritors of archaeological texts and past producers of those utterances, and contemporary colleagues in the critical work of understanding what it is to be an archaeologist. While the multiple dialogues presented here thus intentionally strive to encompass a diverse array of relations of space, time, and situation, equally true to the concerns of Bakhtin, we make no claim to exhaust the potential of this dialogue. This text is closed only as a physical object held in your hands. The voices it contains will continue to engage in dialogues with other voices, including yours, in the open-ended, unfinalizable production of meaning.

1

Introducing the First Voice

Seeking the Thread: Archaeology as Storytelling

At a dinner arranged by a friend, I listened with delight to a senior colleague, a principal authority on the oral traditions of a South American indigenous group. I had never met my dinner companion before, and had only his previous writings to frame my expectations. These were scholarly works in the best university tradition, and included editions of the major creation myths told by the indigenous group.

I listened fascinated as our senior colleague described how the goal of publishing these stories required him and his collaborators to follow the single "thread" that continued through what in actual performance was a dynamic, dialogic storytelling event. As he described it, members of the community gathered to hear the storyteller recount a familiar epic, but far from listening passively, they directed the storyteller's account through their own interventions. My colleague described people asking for specific episodes that they enjoyed, and challenging the storyteller's version, "reminding" the narrator of details he did not include, sometimes picking up the story themselves to set the record straight (compare Norrick 1997). All this dynamic ended up filtered out, in pursuit of the narrative line, the thread of a continuous, common account of the past.

Archaeology at its best is like the event of storytelling that my colleague described. Our published accounts are woefully inadequate at conveying the actual contingency and dialogue that underlies every statement we make.

That archaeological *writing* is storytelling is a commonplace observation by now, although it continues to be resisted. I would like to suggest that even archaeologists most sympathetic to this point have for the most part overlooked the storytelling that is purely internal to our discipline and that precedes the formalization of stories in lectures, books, museum exhibitions, videos, or electronic media. Fieldwork is not a simple process of transcription of what is in the ground, a transcription that might be expected to have some stability across observers (compare Gero 1996, Hodder 1999: 66–70, 80–98). Fieldwork (like lab work and other forms of archaeological transcription) involves a negotiation of meaning, a re-presentation of some things in the present as traces of other things in the past. Again, this is archaeological commonplace. But who negotiates meaning, and with whom, and how?

In 1994, as a crew of undergraduates, graduate students, and local laborers with multiple seasons of excavation experience worked under the direction of a colleague and myself at a site in northern Honduras, strange traces of burned earth, polished clay, contrasts in texture, and minor inclusions emerged all around us. The excavators acted as sculptors, freeing an image from within the mass, in their confrontation with the low, tell-like site, which had already been extensively altered by earth-moving machinery before we arrived. My codirector and I encouraged our students to formally recognize anything they felt was distinctive in their transcriptions of the traces in the ground into two-dimensional records, and to defer concern with the final decision about whether certain differences made a difference or not. In practice, what this meant was that each move became debatable; undergraduate participants and graduate staff both engaged in questioning what they were seeing, and whether there "really" were differences. No amount of urging that any perceptible and describable change could be acknowledged could override the belief on the part of the student participants that part of their job was to discard some differences *from the beginning*. In this, I submit, our student participants were conforming to the genre of fieldwork, a genre that carries with it the notion that excavators flag meaningful "features" at a low level of interpretation, but still as the result of an interpretation. Our failure to compel an alternative procedure was not mysterious, because our students were engaged in a dialogue with much more authoritative voices than ours. They were negotiating these decisions not (primarily) with us, nor with each other, but with the history of the discipline as they heard it.

And we, of course, were doing the same. Our unique task in the division of field labor was the assessment of the differences recognized by our student participants and their rejoining in Harris matrices interpreting the depositional history of the site. The dialogic character of this process was inescapable because we are codirectors, and thus give literal voice to different arguments: but like our students, part of what we uttered were disembodied voices from our disciplinary pasts. One day, contemplating a U-shaped, fire-hardened feature in the wall of a road-cut, I heard myself virtually chanting the list of possible identifications: "It could be the vent of a kiln, like the one I excavated at Travesía, but that one didn't slope. Didn't Doris Stone report some strange tubular features next to one of the small platforms she described at Travesía?"

These were the fragments of storytelling that would, in other circumstances, without a literal audience, simply have run through my mind. They were like in kind to the fragmentary storytelling in which our student participants engaged as they struggled to make their own decisions to recognize their own perceptions as real. And our student participants expected that one of our roles would be to arbitrate, to guide their own murmuring by connecting it to voices from the disciplinary past, like those that run constantly through my consciousness when I am at work.

Like the retelling of the oral histories of South American peoples by the senior folklorist in my opening anecdote, archaeological work begins with storytelling, and the clamor of a multitude of voices goes into the final consistent thread we trace. Contemporary normative expectations of archaeological genres erase the dialogic production of knowledge in favor of images of hierarchically structured authority. These hierarchies lead not only to local, current authorities – field directors, lab directors, authors, and senior authors – but to the weight of what has traditionally been thought and "known". Archaeology as storytelling is intertextual, and like other forms of intertextual narrative, it has always been collaborative and dialogic.

Archaeology: Writing and Language

James Deetz (1988a: 15–20), following Walter Taylor (1948: 34–5), has drawn attention to an ambiguity of the term "archaeology," which subsumes two different sets of practices. On one hand, the word conjures up images of the fieldworker (less commonly, lab worker) discovering the material traces of past societies. In this sense, archaeology is the capturing of data by uniquely qualified leaders of campaigns (chapter 2). But archaeology is also the covering term for "the writing of contexts from the material culture of past actuality" (Deetz 1988: 18). Deetz, and Taylor before him, sought to draw much-needed attention to the duality of the meaning of "archaeology" in order to insist that the writing of archaeology was as integral to the production of archaeological knowledge as encounters in the field (see also Deetz 1989, Baker, Taylor, and Thomas 1990, Sinclair 1989).

While endorsing the importance of such self-consciousness, I also suggest in the pages that follow that the use of a single term for both aspects of archaeological knowledge construction reveals something fundamental about the inseparability of these different practices for the discipline. Writing pervades archaeology, from the creation of field notes and other records of research observations to the creation of informal and formal presentations. Archaeology is continually being scripted and rescripted from previous fragments, both in these writing practices and in its other embodied activities. The acts of recognition through which we identify particular material traces as evidence to be recorded, prior to their inscription, are bound up in the dialogic production of narrative. Via this process an archaeologist engages, more or less consciously, in dialogues with the prior utterances of other archaeological subjects (chapter 3). The representation in written texts of the constant dialogic transactions that actually constitute archaeology as a field (discipline) should not obscure the fact that each text is simply a material form for one segment of the ongoing narrative crafting of disciplinary objects and disciplinary subjects (chapter 4). The production and circulation of physical texts is in part a material means to mark out the boundaries of archaeology as a field (of discourse). Increasingly, archaeological practitioners have been forced to recognize the permeability of these boundaries and the ways archaeological dialogues echo beyond them (chapter 5).

The dual sense of "archaeology," then, requires simultaneous consideration of all the embodied acts through which archaeological knowledge is constructed, including the writing of archaeological texts. In the pages that follow, I suggest that the conceptual vocabulary and approach of Mikhail Bakhtin can help clarify questions of how and why multiple-voiced stories created in the act of archaeology are simplified in the writing of archaeological texts, and why it matters that archaeologists attempt to recapture the multi-voicedness of the experience of constructing archaeological knowledge (chapter 6).

Michael Holquist (1990: 14–15) characterizes the binding element in the highly complex and diverse work of Mikhail Bakhtin as "a pragmatically oriented theory of knowledge; . . . one of several modern epistemologies that seek to grasp human behavior through the use humans make of language. Bakhtin's distinctive place among these is specified by the dialogic concept of language he proposes as

fundamental." Dialogue is the concept Bakhtin employs when speaking of the formation of the self, which occurs only through engagement with an other (Todorov 1984: 29–34, Holquist 1990: 21–33).
Through the concept of "answerability" Bakhtin (1993) presents dialogue as essentially ethical. Bakhtin developed his concept of dialogue
most completely in his studies of the novel (Bakhtin 1981, 1984).
These works are not unrelated to the project of understanding the
creation of narratives in archaeology, a point I will return to below.
But Bakhtin also explored the implications of dialogue for the human
sciences, discussions which directly underwrite the use I make of his
work in this book.

In "Toward a Methodology for the Human Sciences," Bakhtin
(1986: 161) writes:

> The exact sciences constitute a monologic form of knowledge: the intel-
> lect contemplates a *thing* and expounds upon it. There is only one
> subject here – cognizing (contemplating) and speaking (expounding).
> In opposition to the subject there is only a *voiceless thing*. Any object
> of knowledge (including [a human being]) can be perceived and cog-
> nized as a thing. But a subject as such cannot be perceived and studied
> as a thing, for as a subject it cannot, while remaining a subject, become
> voiceless, and consequently, cognition of it can only be *dialogic*.

Dialogue here has a particular meaning: "double-voicedness" (see
Bakhtin 1981: 434, 1984: 185–6):

> No living word relates to its object in a *singular* way: between the word
> and its object, between the word and the speaking subject, there exists
> an elastic environment of other, alien words about the same object, the
> same theme. . . . Any concrete discourse (utterance) finds the object at
> which it was directed already as it were overlain with qualifications,
> open to dispute, charged with value, already enveloped in an obscur-
> ing mist – or, on the contrary, by the "light" of alien words that have
> already been spoken about it. It is entangled, shot through with shared
> thoughts, points of view, alien value judgements and accents. (Bakhtin
> 1981: 276)

Todorov (1984: 49–56) argues that Bakhtin's notion of discourse as
dialogue or double-voicedness is based on seeing language as a relation between, at a minimum, three parties: the speaker, the listener to
whom the utterance is addressed, and an other or others who have
already used the words employed and in the process endowed them
with the quality of double-voicedness, of already having been made
meaningful. Bakhtin's dialogue requires a society of speakers and the

listeners they address in expectation of receiving a response, which always evaluates, critiques, confirms, contests, or reinflects the received utterance.

The dialogic model consequently requires the assumption of a complex model of communication and meaning-making which, I suggest, is particularly appropriate for contemporary archaeology. In particular, it offers an alternative to the either/or of structural abstraction or individualism. In "Discourse in the Novel" Bakhtin (1981: 269–80) proposes his notion of double-voicedness in direct contrast to structuralist and formalist linguistic theory, which he indicts for conceiving of language only at either the level of a whole system or of an individual producing monologic utterances. Instead, he argues that it is imperative to understand that language derives meaning in utterances which are dialogic, taking place between speaking subjects and addressed, and thus potentially answering, subjects:

> The word [discourse] (or in general any sign) is interindividual. . . . The word [discourse] cannot be assigned to a single speaker. The author (speaker) has his own inalienable right to the word [discourse], but the listener also has his rights, and those whose voices are heard in the word before the author comes upon it also have their rights. . . . The word [discourse] is a drama in which three characters participate. (Bakhtin 1986: 121–2; alternatives in brackets after Todorov 1984: 52)

Todorov (1984: 94–112) insists particularly on the importance in Bakhtin's thought of the dialogic other, who is necessary for the completion of the self and the creation of meaning in texts. Dialogue is opposed to monologism:

> Monologism, at its extreme, denies the existence outside itself of another consciousness with equal rights and responsibilities, another *I* with equal rights (*thou*). With a monologic approach (in its extreme or pure form) *another person* remains wholly and merely an *object* of consciousness, and not another consciousness. No response is expected from it that could change everything in the world of my consciousness. Monologue is finalized and deaf to the other's response, does not expect it and does not acknowledge in it any *decisive* force. Monologue manages without the other, and therefore to some degree materializes [objectivizes] all reality. Monologue pretends to be the *ultimate word*. It closes down the represented world and represented persons. (Bakhtin 1984: 292–3; alternatives in brackets after Todorov 1984: 107)

A dialogic perspective, consequently, is especially apt for the attempt to represent some degree of autonomy of human subjects in the texts created in the human sciences (Bakhtin 1986: 103–31). It is also a useful way to place specific texts in their disciplinary context and acknowledge their lack of closure:

> The transcription of thinking in the human sciences is always the tran-
> scription of a special kind of dialogue: the complex interrelations
> between the *text* (the object of study and reflection) and the created,
> framing *context* (questioning, refuting, and so forth) in which the
> scholar's cognizing and evaluating thought takes place. This is the
> meeting of two texts – of the ready-made and the reactive text being
> created – and, consequently, the meeting of two subjects and two
> authors. (Bakhtin 1986: 106–7)

The "ready-made" texts of the human sciences are explicitly defined as including "any coherent complex of signs," including performed gestures (Bakhtin 1986: 103, 106), a point to which we will return.

Dialogue is the overarching concept that pervades Bakhtin's work. It is so central and multiple in its meanings (Morson and Emerson 1990: 49–52) that it is apt to slip through our fingers. The means through which dialogue is realized are, in contrast, somewhat easier to define and identify in practice. Key concepts are heteroglossia and polyphony. All words, all speech, all utterances, come to hand already endowed with the "light" of use in other contexts. Heteroglossia, the term used to translate the Russian word employed by Bakhtin (1981: 428), refers to the presence in "any single national language" of multiple speech types, "social dialects, characteristic group behavior, professional jargons, generic languages, languages of generations and age groups, tendentious languages, languages of the authorities, of various circles and of passing fashions, languages that serve the specific sociopolitical purposes of the day, even of the hour," an "internal stratification" specific to a particular place and time (Bakhtin 1981: 262–3). This stratification of any single language is intentionally employed in performance, and in transcription in texts, to convey meaning, and is integral to the communicative event represented by an oral or written utterance (Bakhtin 1981: 288–96). Contemporary archaeology is experiencing particularly intense heteroglossia, with its multiple scientific dialects juxtaposed to the highly charged common-language meanings of words (particularly words like history, culture, race, and origin) and the resignification of both technical and common-language words in heteroglossic use within different communities to which archaeology is meaningful.

One of the goals of the chapters that follow is to identify and illustrate the stratification of the languages of archaeology in contemporary practice. Another is to examine how various authors have responded to the recognition of archaeological heteroglossia in their own production of new texts. Particularly interesting in this regard are self-conscious attempts by some archaeologists to engage others across the stratification of language (for example, Bender 1998). Bakhtin (1984) coined the term "polyphony" for the representation of multiple distinct languages (heteroglossia) with equal integrity, in his study of Dostoevsky's novels. Within archaeology, experiments with similar aims have more commonly used the term "multivocality" (see the comments by Ruth Tringham in Bender 1998: 86–7; compare Hodder 1999: 159–61, 173, 183, 195). Multivocality will be retained here as the term for the archaeological practice whose goal is to achieve Bakhtin's polyphony.

The differentiation of heteroglossia and polyphony in Bakhtin's work underlines the necessity to examine whether multivocality in archaeology truly incorporates significant degrees of difference in language, or simply represents multiple instances of the same language assigned to multiple versions of the author. Polyphonic narratives are marked by the autonomy and strength of the voices, which are represented as engaged in open-ended dialogue where ultimate values are in play but necessarily cannot be finalized. If the multiple voices in a polyphonic text are not at least potentially capable of achieving a degree of autonomy that engages their difference in dialogue, then in place of polyphony the text offers only an image of repeated monologues. The goal of multivocality in archaeology has been to achieve polyphony, but this has not always been the outcome (Pluciennik 1999: 667).

The distinction between heteroglossia and polyphony is also crucial to the project of recovering the already existing multiplicity of languages that even the most univocal archaeological texts incorporate. Archaeology does not operate in isolation from other heteroglossic languages, and it has always worked to embed its own specific dialects in dialogue with other prestige and common languages. The language of positivist science that Americanist archaeology borrowed in the 1960s is only one very obvious example of this kind of engagement (Binford 1968, Fritz and Plog 1970; see Wylie in press: Chs 3–4). The programmatic texts which called for hypothesis-testing and the construction of general covering laws, while in no obvious way polyphonic, were intensely heteroglossic: the words employed had already been given meaning and value in other narratives, and their reproduction as indirect and direct cited speech in archaeological texts engaged their users in other dialogues. The use of conceptual terms from outside archaeology by post-processual authors like Shanks and Tilley (1987) can be seen as a repetition of the introduction of a new external language into archaeology.

The new heteroglossia distinctive of post-processual archaeology was well understood by critics as marking out an oppositional community based on the ability to speak a specific dialect. Yoffee and Sherratt's (1993: 5–6) characterization of this move as "mining" other fields can perhaps be viewed as an embodiment of a desire for a separate archaeological "national" language (in Bakhtin's terms) in which meaning would be independent of other languages. But while the heteroglossia of the self-conscious programmatic writing of processual and post-processual archaeologists may be overtly obvious, heteroglossia is inescapable so long as the words we use circulate in and out of society at large. "The author (speaker) has his own inalienable right to the word, but the listener also has his rights, and those whose voices are heard in the word before the author comes upon it also have their rights" (Bakhtin 1986: 121).

Archaeology: Dialogue–Narrative–Text

Bakhtin's theoretical vocabulary has been widely used in literary studies to examine fictional texts, as well as in the analysis of the texts created by social or natural scientists to represent their understandings of the nonfictional phenomena they study (see Billig 1993, Hill 1995, Mandelker 1995, Mannheim and Tedlock 1995, McDermott and Tylbor 1995, Tannen 1995, Trawick 1988, Weiss 1990). If, following Hayden White (1987: 44–46), we allow that the boundary between fictional texts and historiographic texts is less impermeable than sometimes proposed, it is possible to use the experience of literary critics with Bakhtinian concepts as a guide to their utility in examining archaeological narrative (see also Price 1999: 19–34). To do so requires some beginning discrimination of narrative from discourse, dialogue, and text.

> In the most general terms, to narrate is to tell a story . . . narration of any kind involves the recounting and shaping of events . . . narration has an essential temporal dimension . . . narrative imposes structure; it connects as well as records . . . Finally, for every narrative, there is a narrator, real or implied or both. Stories don't just exist, they are told, and not just told but told from some perspective or other. Already we have four basic dimensions of all narrative: time, structure, voice, and point of view. (Lamarque 1990: 131)

White (1987: 2) espouses a relatively restricted definition of narrative, as a story with a beginning, middle, and end, in support of his general argument that historical narratives in this strict sense are always products of, and arguments for, some threatened social order. Some aspects of his discussion of these concomitants of historical narratives are particularly useful for a consideration of archaeological texts, and will return in the dialogues that follow. Most useful is his distinction between historical narratives (stories) and narrativizing (telling), based on the work of Gérard Genette (1980, 1988). White cites a discussion by Genette of Emile Benveniste's contrast between *histoire* and *discours*, in which Genette argued that *histoire* is distinguished by "the exclusive use of the third person and of such forms as the preterite and the pluperfect," through which the "objectivity of narrative is defined by the absence of all reference to the narrator" (White 1987: 2–3). Thus for White, the historical narrative is specifically that of an apparently objective speaker recounting what happened: beginning, middle, and end.

While useful for White's purposes, this particular formulation is almost the reverse of Genette's general model of narrative, which is fundamental to the present study. Genette (1988: 13–14) distinguishes between story (narrated events), narrative (the oral or written discourse that tells events), and narration (the act of telling events). He specifically repudiates his own collapse of Benveniste's *histoire* into narrative (*récit*). Genette emphasizes the inseparability of the three terms he employs – story, narrative, and narration – in specific contrast to the Russian Formalist dichotomy story/plot (Propp 1968), which has been the touchstone for pioneering studies of narrative in physical anthropology (Landau 1991) and archaeology (Pluciennik 1999). Genette (1988: 14–15) suggests that in historical narrative "the actual order is obviously *story* (the completed events), *narrating* (the narrative act of the historian), *narrative*." That "obviously" is immediately challenged: "But has a pure fiction ever existed? And a pure nonfiction? The answer in both cases is obviously negative" (Genette 1988: 15). Genette proceeds to distinguish between clearly fictional and nonfictional narratives, not in terms of grammatical voice or tense, but in terms of substantiation *by an auditor/reader*: "the typically modal query 'How does the author know that?' does not have the same meaning in fiction as in nonfiction. In nonfiction, the historian must provide evidence and documents . . ." (Genette 1988: 15).

This formulation recalls Bakhtin's (1993: 1–2, 8–19) comments about the relation between always-ongoing Being-as-Event and its representations, in which representation cannot be set free from events. The closed nature of historical narrative, as White defines it, and as conceived of in most historiographic writing, is intensely problematic to the extent that the narrative claims to be an accurate or truthful account (in Bakhtin's 1993: 4–5 terms, "veridical"). One advantage of the Bakhtinian conceptual approach adopted here is that it insists that relative truthfulness does matter, through the concept of *answerability* (Bakhtin 1993: 2–428–9). The Russian word used can also be translated as *responsibility*, implying both the demand that dialogue makes for a response, and the ethical weight of making a response (Holquist 1990: 152–5, Morson and Emerson 1990: 25–7). Over Bakhtin's career, his concerns moved from discussions more consistent with the translation "responsibility" to those concerned with the demand for a reply, but even in these latter, more literary formulations, the concept of responsibility for *making* a reply and for the *nature* of that reply was retained (Morson and Emerson 1990: 76).

Bakhtin rejected extreme relativist and determinist positions concerning history as literally irresponsible, and demanded that history be considered as both open, or unfinalizable, and still partly ordered (Morson and Emerson 1990: 43–9). I will consider implications of this insistence on the underdetermined nature of each moment for the creation of archaeological narratives in later chapters. For now, it is most important to note that use of Bakhtin's framework requires that archaeologists treat the choice of specific stories about the past as having real consequences for which we are responsible, because our narratives are addressed dialogically to another whose reaction we intend to provoke. A similar point is made by White (1987: 26–57), who argues that historical narratives, as they transform events into story, do so in a way that is given meaning through deliberate evocation of evaluative responses colored by experience of specific generic literary forms. "The historical narrative does not, as narrative, dispel false beliefs about the past, human life, the nature of the community, and so on; what it does is test the capacity of a culture's fictions to endow real events with the kinds of meaning that literature displays" (White 1987: 45).

White's concept of the historical narrative is obviously useful in beginning to raise issues archaeology must also address. Equally relevant is work on narrative by Roland Barthes, to which White (1987: 1–2, 35, 37–8, 42–3) refers. Barthes (1977c) provided a fully-developed structuralist methodology for the analysis of narratives in written texts, including historical texts (Barthes 1981), that proposed crucial relationships between the writer and reader. For Barthes, the meaning in narrative texts was immanent but not closed; the writer's work shaped a potential which the reader invoked by acts of recognition. The reader's experience and knowledge threaded through the text, promoting its understanding as a story. Bakhtin argued that structuralist and semiotic accounts that reduced communication to encoding and decoding meanings were fundamentally flawed (Morson and Emerson 1990: 50–1, 57–8). To the extent that we can take Barthes to be describing a manner of engagement through texts that produced meaning, rather than a methodology based on "decoding" finalized meanings encoded in texts by authors, his work is compatible with that of Bakhtin, who can be considered to be advocating a practice- or performance-based form of semiotics (Jefferson 1989, Danow 1991: 10, 34–5).

The texts Barthes examined conform generally to White's definition of a narrative as having a beginning, middle, and end. They do so not solely because they were constructed in that form by their author, but because the reader completes the story through his or her reading; a narrative ends because the reader provides it a provisional finality. A similar provisional finalization, conceived of as one of many possible finalities, all constrained by the text and so in no way subject to an absolute relativism, was called for in Bakhtin's discussions of the responsibility of acting in the world (Morson and Emerson 1990: 70–1). Texts or utterances were, or should be, absolutely unfinalizable, from the dialogic perspective, because they always call for a response. At the same time, each person is required to make unique, unrepeatable responses that *are* finalized, through the concrete context within which they take place. Each utterance opens up broad possibilities of response; each response made from and in a specific historical place is a unique and unrepeatable event. Utterances are parts of ongoing dialogue; acts are unique local events through which someone claims responsibility for understanding and answering an utterance. Barthes describes acts through which provisional meanings immanent in texts are finalized, but none of the acts he describes should be seen as anything other than specific situated instances of narration. There are no grounds to privilege one reading beforehand (Olsen 1990; compare Owoc 1989).

Barthes (1977b, 1977d) adds an important dimension to an understanding of archaeological narratives not provided by any of Bakhtin's writings in his consideration of visual representations. Archaeological utterances are often composed of symbolic forms other than words. Photographs and drawings cannot meaningfully be described as having a beginning, middle, and end; instead they present themselves as tableaux, frozen or pregnant moments (Barthes 1977b: 73).

Simultaneity replaces linearity and the viewer's active role in constructing narratives is potentially much more obvious than when text alone is at issue. Barthes demonstrates that the resources brought to bear in constructing narratives from visual images are drawn from the previous experience of the viewer. Because individual experience is diverse, what Bakhtin would call the context of each dialogic moment of narrative production is open: all images are polysemous; they imply, underlying their signifiers, a 'floating chain' of signifieds, the reader able to choose some and ignore others" (Barthes 1977d: 38–9). In Bakhtin's terms, the viewer of an image responds to the call for an answer on the part of the voice embodied in the image. In Barthes's terms, this response takes the form of creating a narrative in which the image is one moment. For Bakhtin, the context of response by any viewer will be unique, and so will the provisional finalization provided by a particular narrative.

Both Barthes and Bakhtin are concerned with the way that open-ended construction of meaning avoids complete singularity. For Barthes (1972), the predictability of response is something deliberately shaped, a nexus of the exercise of power, as for example by political regimes or capitalist enterprises. For Bakhtin, the repeatable shape of a response stems from the heteroglossia of the forms that carry meaning, which have already accumulated meanings that inflect their reading. For both, the possibility that recipients of utterances (verbal or visual) will provide responses similar to those expected by the speaker is a reflection of shared experience, shared context, and shared knowledge. Understanding simultaneously shapes a community and relies on an already existing sharing, although in neither case is this sharing an identity. For Bakhtin, in fact, the condition required for communication is nonidentity.

Otherness and Archaeological Authors

Bakhtin was concerned with exploring the ambiguous position of the author, as someone charged with creating a provisionally finalized work. Morson and Emerson (1990: 179–86) suggest that Bakhtin was concerned with the ethical dimensions of authoring as part of the formation of the self. Fundamental to this concern was a rejection of traditional subject–object dualism, in favor of a relational process through which the self and other were mutually constituted. This relational process is founded on perception of the self as triadic: I-for-myself, I-for-others ("outsideness"), and the-other-for-me ("otherness"). An awareness of irresolvable difference between oneself and another is required for there to be an awareness of an authentic self.

For archaeological authors, perhaps the most crucial implication of Bakhtin's arguments in this regard is his insistence that we cannot place ourselves in the position of the other (compare Thomas 1990). Bakhtin critiques various forms of attempted pretense of otherness as irresponsible aestheticization of other subjects, transforming them into mere mirrors for our self, "pretender-doubles" or "soul-slaves." He equally condemns the conversion of the self into a representation of a larger whole, sacrificing the irreducible experience of subjectivity for the power of speaking for others. Morson and Emerson (1990: 183) write that for Bakhtin theories "based on collapsing many consciousnesses into a single abstract generalizable consciousness miss the whole point" of authoring; "for Bakhtin, whatever serves to 'fuse' serves to impoverish because it destroys outsideness and otherness." Because he is concerned with precisely the tension between the work authors do and the degree to which they can, in that work, absorb other subjects, Bakhtin's approach provides a uniquely useful way to think about the challenges of contemporary archaeological writing. His work has the potential to help support evaluation of different archaeological narratives according to new criteria, based neither on asserted authority nor on unbelievable claims of certainty, criteria that are compatible both with a call for multiple perspectives and with a desire to evaluate the effects of different stories in the world.

These arguments will return in the following pages. First, however, we will need to explore further the narrative production of archaeological knowledge. Archaeology is a storytelling discipline from its inception in the field or lab. Its linear written texts can only be understood as part of ongoing dialogues that began aurally and experientially. The starting point for those dialogues, and the point to which archaeology recurs in practice and rhetorically, is the field, the site of discovery. But what, precisely, is the field in archaeology?

2

Writing the Field of Archaeology

First Dialogue: Feminism, Fieldwork, and the Practice of Archaeology[1]

Rosemary A. Joyce with Robert W. Preucel

It has been said that the person with a clear objective and a plan of campaign is more likely to succeed than the average person with neither, and this is certainly true of archaeology. The military overtones of the words *"objective"* and *"campaign"* are entirely appropriate for archaeology, which often requires the recruitment, funding, and coordination of large numbers of people in complex field projects. It is no accident that two pioneers of field techniques – Pitt-Rivers and Mortimer Wheeler – were old soldiers. Renfrew and Bahn (1991: 61)

From: preucel@xxxx.xxxxxxx.edu

Date: 26 Nov 94 17:10:05 EST

To: joyce@xxxxx.xxxxxxxx.edu

Subject: Re: AAA Paper

Dear Rosy,

It's getting time to begin working on our paper looking at the relationships between Feminism, Fieldwork, and Archaeological Practice. I really like your idea about organizing our presentation around our three related themes: fieldwork as a social practice, the gendering of fieldwork as male, and the reconstitution of fieldwork in ways that might be more inclusive of women and more representative of all archaeological practice. Here are some of my thoughts on the first two.

Fieldwork is traditionally regarded as that portion of archaeological activity dedicated to the discovery of archaeological sites though survey and the exploration of some of those sites by excavation. It is uniquely responsible for the acquisition of archaeological data, e.g., artifacts, ecofacts, and features. This association is so strong that archaeology is widely considered to be synonymous with excavation. Metonymically, the part stands for the whole.

Fieldwork, more than any other activity, then, occupies a privileged position. We are constantly being asked by our colleagues and the public alike: Where do we dig? What is our most recent discovery? How much dirt have we moved? And on and on. The question we have not thought to ask ourselves is why is this so? Why is excavation valued over other kinds of data-gathering activities such as laboratory analysis or museum studies? It seems to me that we can begin to construct an answer, if we consider fieldwork more as a social practice than a scientific methodology.

On this account, fieldwork both constitutes and reproduces archaeology as a profession. It is a means of defining disciplinary boundaries. Archaeology, for example, is different from geology, another field science, by virtue of its specialized methodologies and language. Fieldwork acts as a rite of passage. We require all students to gain first-hand experience though an apprenticeship with a trained professional, and this usually takes place in a field-school setting. Finally, it is a mark of status. We evaluate each other on the basis of the number of different projects we have been associated with throughout our careers.

Now given this social aspect, it is particularly interesting to look at how fieldwork has come to be gendered male. We now know something of the historical dimensions of this process as a result of the growing body of feminist scholarship in archaeology. Your study of Dorothy Popenoe shows how she was forced to chart her career at the margins of the profession by the male academic establishment. My work with Meredith Chesson on Isabel Kelly suggests much the same. And Meg Conkey's and Joan Gero's work has given us some preliminary statistics that suggest that contemporary archaeological fieldwork is still disproportionately dominated by males.[2]

What we still don't fully understand are the ways in which we perpetuate this exclusion. How is it that women are being made to feel incompetent or unqualified to conduct fieldwork? I have found Donna Haraway's work particularly enlightening in this

before 1900	Sir W. M. Flinders Petrie, 1883, *Ten Years' Digging in Egypt.* General Pitt-Rivers, 1887, 1888, 1892, 1898, *Excavations in Cranborne Chase.* Vols. 1–4
1900–20	J. P. Droop, 1915, *Archaeological Excavation.* Cambridge University Press, Cambridge. Sir W. M. Flinders Petrie, 1904, *Methods and Aims in Archaeology.* London.
1921–45	Sir Leonard Woolley, 1930, *Digging Up the Past.* Ernest Benn Ltd. London.
1946–60	R. J. C. Atkinson, 1946, *Field Archaeology.* V. Gordon Childe, 1956, *A Short Introduction to Archaeology.* Robert F. Heizer, ed., 1949, *A Manual of Archaeological Field Methods.* The National Press, Palo Alto. 1950, *A Manual of Archaeological Field Methods.* 2nd edition. The National Press, Palo Alto. 1953, *A Manual of Archaeological Field Methods.* 3rd edition. The National Press, Palo Alto. Kathleen Kenyon, 1952, *Beginning in Archaeology.* Sir Mortimer Wheeler, 1954, *Archaeology From the Earth.* Oxford University Press, Oxford. 1955, *Still Digging: Interleaves from an Antiquary's Notebook.* Michael Joseph, London. Sir Leonard Woolley, 1953, *Spadework.* Lutterworth Press, London.
1960–80	Robert F. Heizer and John A. Graham, 1967, *A Guide to Field Methods in Archaeology: Approaches to the Anthropology of the Dead.* National Press, Palo Alto. Robert F. Heizer, Thomas N. Hester, and John A. Graham, 1975, *Field Methods in Archaeology.* 6th edition. Mayfield, Palo Alto. Ivor Noel Hume, 1968, *Historical Archaeology.* Alfred Knopf, New York. Martha Joukowsky, 1980, *A Complete Manual of Field Archaeology: Tools and Techniques of Field Work for Archaeologists.* Prentice-Hall, Englewood Cliffs, N. J. Robert Sharer and Wendy Ashmore, 1979, *Fundamentals of Archaeoology.* Benjamine Cummings, Menlo Park. 1987, *Archaeology: Discovering our Past.* Mayfield, Palo Alto. David Hurst Thomas, 1979, *Archaeology.* Holt, Rinehart and Winston, New York. Sir Leonard Woolley, 1962, *History Unearthed.*
1981–2001	Thomas N. Hester, H. J. Shafer, and Robert F. Heizer, 1987, *Field Methods in Archaeology.* Mayfield, Palo Alto. Colin Renfrew and Paul Bahn, 1991, *Archaeology: Theories, Methods, and Practice.* Thames and Hudson, London. Robert Sharer and Wendy Ashmore, 1993, *Archaeology: Discovering our Past.* 2nd edition, Mayfield, Palo Alto. David Hurst Thomas, 1989, *Archaeology.* 2nd edition, Holt, Rinehart and Winston, New York.

Figure 2.1 *Distribution over time of introductory texts consulted in the survey*

regard. She says that the discourses of modern primatology "participate in the preeminent political act of western history, namely the construction of Man." She shows that primatology constitutes its object of knowledge through metaphoric systems that both structure observations and serve to interpret them. This suggests that one way we might understand the exclusion of women is to examine the metaphors we use when we talk about fieldwork.[3]

Along with two research assistants (Meredith Chesson and Erika Evasdottir), I have begun a survey of 30 introductory archaeology textbooks spanning a period of over one hundred years (figure 2.1). All but three were written by male authors. We have limited our review to English language publications because we are more familiar with the construction of gender ideologies in British and American contexts. We expect that our results will be relevant to non-English-speaking countries (especially countries touched by Anglo-American colonialism), although each case will likely require modifications appropriate to specific cultural contexts.

Our survey has revealed a wide variety of metaphors, but one metaphor, in particular, stands out and deserves the designation as a guiding metaphor or core narrative because of its consistent use throughout the period of study. This is the comparison of archaeological fieldwork to war!

Fieldwork is portrayed as a military campaign. The words and phrases used are such things as: tactics, strategy, reconnaissance, point of attack, line of command, troops, field of action, and battle. The earliest example is Sir Flinders Petrie (1904), who talks about methods of "attacking" a large site. A recent example is the discussion of "objective" and plan of "campaign" in Colin Renfrew and Paul Bahn's popular text (1991).

Two results are particularly interesting. The first is that Wheeler and his contemporaries originally justified the use of the military metaphor on scientific grounds! The idea is that archaeologists should have a clear objective, and a well-defined plan of action. The metaphor is particularly well developed in terms of a hierarchy of personnel each with specific tasks, the assumption being that excavations must be organized in an efficient fashion in order to produce reliable results. This emphasis on the scientific method was widely adopted to set off archaeology from antiquarian dabbling.

The second is that the military metaphor explicitly genders the field archaeologist as male. The ideal director should possess the same qualities as a military leader. These are, according to Noel Hume (1968: 54), "a thorough knowledge of how the job should be done, the ability to delegate authority, a personality capable of evoking comradeship and respect from his team, and an ability to imbue enthusiasm into others." The ideal fieldworker should embody the characteristics of an infantryman. Atkinson (1946: 64), for example, writes of "the navvy (a male laborer) as the proper worker for the archaeological dig because he is strong, efficient, enduring, and follows orders."

This military metaphor, its association with the creation of a science of archaeology, and its linkage to a series of related male attributes makes clear some of the ways women have been excluded from fieldwork. Women are actively discouraged from participating in fieldwork on the grounds that they do not possess the attributes of the ideal male fieldworker. But on a more insidious level, they are also discouraged by the language we use when we talk about fieldwork as a military campaign.

Our study suggests that the ways we think about fieldwork still depend to a surprising degree upon the outdated, androcentric twentieth-century ideology of men's and women's roles and capabilities. And as long as we continue to use these military metaphors uncritically we will be complicit in reproducing an environment that is exclusionary of women.

Let me know what you think of these ideas.

Best, Bob

From: joyce@xxxxx.xxxxxxxx.edu (Rosemary Joyce)

Date: Mon, 28 Nov 94 19:32:40 PST

To: preucel@xxxxx.xxxxxxxx.edu

Subject: Re: AAA Paper-Exchange on First Theme

Dear Bob,

I am encouraged that you have found such a clear thread of gender in the historical metaphors for fieldwork. To the extent that we continue to foster this language, and equally important, the practices that it legitimates, clearly doing fieldwork well is a masculine activity. Your findings about military models and metaphors also suggest to me some clarification of aspects of talk about fieldwork that I find somewhat puzzling.

You mention, for example, the way that within the profession we often engage in talk about "moving dirt." To that I would add a whole series of subjects that concern the obstacles that are overcome in real fieldwork: the primitive conditions that seem to be an implicit norm, for example, that lead those privileged to work in first-world countries to apologize for the way work is eased. Certainly, I have found myself on any number of occasions locked in exchanges about vermin, especially snakes, that seem to have no point other than to establish that the field – as a location for action – was not domesticated.

These kinds of comments seem to stem less from the military code than from something further. They emphasize the personal experience that the fieldworker has endured, the way that fieldwork challenged the individual archaeologist to overcome logistical problems and succeed in finding the data. The most obvious aspect of the fieldworker in this discourse is his (and I do mean his) singularity. Perhaps this stems from the hierarchy explicitly embedded in the military metaphor. You note that our professional status accrues from our fieldwork, creating a status hierarchy; but that status hierarchy itself presupposes the hierarchy of field authority.

I suspect, then, that a byproduct of the construction of fieldwork as a male activity headed by an officer is an emphasis on the experience of that person. Fieldwork essentially has two different products. As an activity that is public, it is meant to produce pasts. But more important within the discipline, fieldwork produces products that are fieldworkers – those who have had revelatory contact with the intransigent remains of the past and wrested them free from their burial matrix.[4]

I cannot escape seeing a familiar archetype here, the Hero Quest as outlined in Propp's study of the folk tale or as popularized by Joseph Campbell. The central figure may be aided in his quest by all manner of supernatural or animal helpers, but he bears the sole responsibility for the outcome of the quest. He brings to bear the tools that his helpers provide, but they cannot effect the resolution of the narrative. As in our disciplinary practice of fieldwork, the Hero Quest has two distinct products: it changes the Hero, giving him a unique authority; and at the same time, his actions result in the capture of a prize.[5]

It seems to me that this emphasis on the singular experience of the classic fieldworker is one source of the resistance we feel toward recognizing the collaborative nature of fieldwork and the equally important contributions that documentary, museum, and lab research make to the construction of archaeological knowledge. Not only are collaborators seen as subordinates in a campaign, they act the role of magical helpers in the quest.

One of the concrete dimensions of fieldwork as classically constituted that is common to both sets of metaphors, and enacted in practice, is the journey to a physical field site. It seems to me that, in order to change our language to authorize less emphasis on hierarchies of value in our research labors, and to legitimate collaborative research without devaluing one of the collaborators, we need to seek out other metaphors for the field. The fringe concepts we already have – solving puzzles, detection, and the like – still suffer from their emphasis on the individual and on the discovery of what was already there. The power of metaphors that have lasted a century is not going to be countered without an equally powerful alternative language.

Best, Rosy

From: preucel@xxxx.xxxxxxx.edu

Date: 26 Nov 94 17:10:05 EST

To: joyce@xxxxx.xxxxxxxx.edu

Subject: Re: AAA Paper

Dear Rosy,

Your discussion of the Hero Quest is fascinating. The archaeologist as Hero who overcomes hardships, journeys to exotic lands, encounters the past as Other. It reminds me that metaphors only exist within plots or narratives, and that there are a number of different narratives at work which together support the androcentric structure of archaeology.

An alternative to the military metaphor that might prove interesting is to think about fieldwork-as-agriculture. This metaphor has the jarring quality that new metaphors tend to have since it juxtaposes two different frames of reference, but it also possesses a certain elegance since its use literally transforms the "field of battle" into the "field of cultivation."

We commonly talk about the seeds of knowledge, harvesting ideas, and cultivating the mind. Cultivation, in fact, was a popular metaphor for the Transcendental philosophers, such as Emerson and Thoreau. This association means that the frames of reference are already familiar to us, thus enhancing its use in another context, in this case an archaeological one.

One important aspect of this metaphor is its potential for creating a new understanding of the production of archaeological knowledge. Agriculture consists of a series of discrete activities including planting, fertilizing, weeding, watering, and harvesting. None of these activities can really be said to be more important than the other; they are all interrelated through biological processes of growth and maturation. Each is necessary in order to accomplish the final result.

Likewise, we might consider fieldwork, not simply as excavation or survey, but rather as a series of activities associated with data collection. This would require revaluing such traditionally marginalized pursuits as library research, laboratory analysis, and the study of museum collections (often the domain of women scholars). Excavation is thus part of the process of knowledge production and on this account of no greater intrinsic value than any other activity.

As Mary Hesse writes, metaphors are potentially revolutionary. So what happens when we change the metaphors of fieldwork? How does it affect how we see women in archaeology? How does it enrich our understanding of the different activities in the production of archaeological knowledge? The point, here, is not to adopt the agriculture metaphor necessarily, but rather to show how metaphors inform how we look at the world, and can be used to effect change.[6]

Best, Bob

From: joyce@xxxxx.xxxxxxxx.edu (Rosemary Joyce)

Date: Mon, 28 Nov 94 19:50:55 PST

To: preucel@xxxxx.xxxxxxxx.edu

Subject: Re: AAA Paper-Exchange on Third Theme

Dear Bob,

Beating our swords into plowshares, metaphorically speaking, seems like a natural recognition of what we already, and increasingly, do. Our fields may be quite varied: some larger, some smaller, some close to home – on-campus field schools as gardens? – and some out at the edge of domesticated space. We can then continue to recognize the very real challenges that going to some field sites presents, without automatically privileging the experience of those who take that step. The evidence of good farming is, after all, found in the harvest.

And as you note, that harvest results from the work of many laborers. More; cultivation is a process that requires bringing different kinds of knowledge to bear at distinct stages, it requires a host of unique activities. If we extend our metaphor to follow the harvest with the processing, then we come closest to really encompassing the way that research requires interdependency of differently skilled and variably engaged workers. I imagine the produce of our archaeological fieldwork as material to be spun into concepts and woven into data structures, the cloth of our arguments ranging from simple homespun to elaborate brocades.

One of the strongest recommendations of this reconstruction of our work is that it still allows us to recognize that there are levels of skill involved in what we do, and that these levels vary with experience. While military metaphors acknowledge the tactical expertise of the general, they provide very poor scope for the idea that footsoldiers actually bring to bear useful insights as they learn from their experience under field direction.

I know that, since we both function in very traditional ways as field directors, we continue to see a need for matching responsibility with experience. But what has been problematic for me as a very traditional field archaeologist has been understanding how to be a collaborator as an equal with the colleagues with whom I codirect my Honduran research. I see my own dilemma as stemming from the way that the male subject position in traditional fieldwork was constituted: not simply as male, but as the leader. It makes no sense to talk about the leader of the farm crew in the same way, but there still is space for experience.

Best, Rosy

Heteroglossia in Archaeology

This *First Dialogue* is an example of collaborative and multivocalic production of knowledge typical of archaeology. Even though it is typical of our processes of knowledge construction, archaeological dialogue is not normally included in the final forms of archaeological texts. I discuss a number of exceptions in the following chapter. Before turning to these counter-examples, a closer reading of the relationship of form and content in the *First Dialogue* will facilitate understanding of a second concept from Bakhtin's philosophy that is highly pertinent to archaeology: heteroglossia.

The heteroglossia of archaeological language is the specific topic of this dialogue. Bakhtin's concept of heteroglossia recognizes that different commonplace languages embedded in speech or writing act like continuing echoes of speakers from the original locations (social classes, performative settings, historical periods, disciplines) where these languages originally gained their currency. Thus, as archaeologists continue, after a century, to use the language first adapted by British gentlemen to characterize their hierarchical experience of directing large-scale field projects, we inevitably engage our contemporary experience in the shades of lived meaning of the earlier use of these terms. Heteroglossia is inherent in the *act*, not merely in its representation. Not only do the *texts* of archaeology present the model of a general marshalling troops, uniquely provided with the perspective to understand the entire campaign; the experience of archaeology through which new practitioners are habituated to the discipline resonates with these same echoes (compare Moser 1996, 1999).

Contemporary archaeology engages with a wide spectrum of languages, and each brings its echoes to the way that both practitioners and others interested in the past understand archaeological utterances. For example, Conkey and Williams (1991) show how origins research in archaeology is shaped by the common meanings of the word "origin." The material traces that archaeologists represent to the public are framed in terms of the beginnings of things understood as a break or invention. Origins research rests on an implication of a gap which Conkey and Williams show is created by the discourse of origins itself. In other words, an originary narrative begins because in the national language the meaning of archaeology is finding the beginnings of things.

The *First Dialogue* documents that one of the languages in wide circulation in archaeology is that of military campaigns. We suggest that another of the languages of archaeology derives from the common folk-tale motifs of the Hero Quest (as Landau 1991 argues for hominid studies). Joan Gero (1983, 1985) has shown that some of the language of North American archaeology derives from talk of the cowboy. The examples can be multiplied, but the main point is made: the words archaeology draws from other commonplace languages echo with meanings that escape our control and shape our communication, both within the discipline and outside it.

As Stephanie Moser (1996, 1999) has shown, initiation into the disciplinary culture of archaeology involves learning a set of values that come embedded in visual and linguistic images. The image of Indiana Jones, examined by both Gero and Moser, draws from an existing language of archaeology – that of the antiquarian collectors generally thought of as inhabiting the late-nineteenth-century history of archaeology – and, revoicing that language, places it in broader circulation as a contemporary image of the archaeologist, even if it is redated as the contemporary Lara Croft, still a privileged individual tomb raider. For a broader public, the authority of the archaeologist thus comes embedded in dialogues of individual, physical effort, usually in exotic locales, through which some form of treasure is gained. The word "archaeology" is embedded in commonplace language as a journey to the field, the site of a dig where discoveries are made. Because of the heteroglossia of national languages, the word archaeology carries echoes of that meaning everywhere it is used, not only in public settings but also in the specialized jargon of the discipline.

Heteroglossia inflects every aspect of archaeology in which communication is at issue. The attempt to shift authority in archaeology to the language of science, promoted in the discipline as part of the New Archaeology of the 1960s and 1970s, drew on the well-established languages of archaeology and science and reaccented both. The requirements of individual effort, still in a relatively exotic locale (even if the exoticism might sometimes be that of the lab as a separate place), and of gaining a treasure were not fundamentally disturbed. Only the goal of the quest changed: no longer literal treasure, but the metaphorical one of knowledge of the laws of human behavior. The languages of science, including the formulation of hypotheses, use of statistical inference, and coining of scientistic terms for objects of study, such as "lithic resource acquisition" instead of "rock use" (Deetz 1998), entered into archaeology and added to its heteroglossia, adding to rather than replacing older languages. The languages of feminism, Marxism, and social theories of subjectivity that entered archaeology as challenges to processualism in the 1980s and 1990s further increased the heteroglossia of the discipline, placing an eclectic array of already-voiced words at the disposal of contemporary archaeologists.

While all of these languages are employed within archaeological practice itself, they simultaneously engage archaeologists in dialogues that extend outside this domain. The scientific pursuits of the 1960s related to philosophies of science based on lab sciences such as physics and chemistry. More recent concerns with feminism, Marxism, and post-structuralism engage with traditional humanities disciplines such as art history, and emerging fields such as visual and cultural studies. When these languages are invoked within archaeology, the statements made are at least partly oriented outward toward these other locations, seeking a response in other dialogues.

Still other aspects of the heteroglossia of contemporary archaeology come from revoicing of archaeological concepts by others outside

the discipline. This is not a new experience, as the use of archaeological findings and terms by nationalist politicians of the early twentieth
century, most notoriously Germany's National Socialists, reminds us
(Arnold 1990, Trigger 1989: 164, 381). What may be new is the degree
to which contemporary archaeologists are aware of the need to participate in dialogues with others. Archaeological accounts revoiced by
nonspecialists can no longer be seen as unconnected with the ongoing
dialogue within the field. The adoption of aspects of European
Neolithic and Palaeolithic archaeology by the Goddess Movement,
for example (Conkey and Tringham 1996, Meskell 1995), cannot be
disclaimed, but must be treated as responses to our attempts to communicate our beliefs about the past. While the specific responses may
have been largely unanticipated, they participate in the reaccenting of
archaeological utterances that shapes the field.

To understand how contemporary archaeologists might better be
able to see themselves engaged in dialogue with nonarchaeologists,
two of Bakhtin's concepts are particularly useful. For Bakhtin, each
utterance (written text or speech act) is part of a communicative event
that incorporates expectations about reception and evaluation. These
communicative events and the dialogues they constitute are unique
and unrepeatable, situated in specific places and times that both lend
to and draw their character from the utterances they encapsulate.
These two concepts – the total context of communication and the
chronotope, the specific "time-place" of communication – are integral to understanding how archaeology shapes itself through dialogue
and narrative.

The Total Context: Communication and Evaluation

Bakhtin (1981: 284, 1986: 75, 105) developed the concept of the "total
context" to account for the complex ways that heteroglossic voices
circulate in both spoken and written dialogues (Morson and Emerson
1990: 126–33, Todorov 1984: 42–51). The total context of an utterance
is what endows it with the specific meaning that, in Bakhtin's view,
is unrepeatable. Although the words employed can be repeated in the
same order, the total context is different, if for no other reason than
because the words have already been said in the first utterance. The
concept of total context is itself dialogic; it includes the knowledge
and understanding common to both parties in an exchange, and their
evaluation (response, answer) to the situation. The shared nature of
the total context is crucial for any communication to take place. And

because of this, utterances always presume an addressee, someone who is expected to respond.

The desire to communicate is fundamental to Bakhtin's concept of speech, and of writing. Communication itself, however, is very different than envisaged in some theories. Bakhtin (1986: 6, 147) explicitly rejects the idea of speakers encoding messages that listeners decode. In his view, this model places all the responsibility for communication on the shoulders of the speaker. Nor does he accept models in which listeners freely interpret what they hear without regard to the speaker. Here again, all the freedom of action, and consequent responsibility, is monopolized by one party, and changing the party does not improve the account. Instead, Bakhtin insists that communication is a social action that binds together speaker and addressee, through the expectation on the part of the speaker of a response from the addressee. This response, according to Bakhtin, is what gives meaning to the speaker's words. It does so by supplying an evaluation of those words, affirming or contesting them.

The total context of communication bears comparison to the "fusion of horizons" critical to hermeneutic approaches in archaeology. Hermeneutics also posits a process of dialogue for the purpose of creating understanding.

> An interpreter aims to provide a reciprocity of understanding, overcoming the lack of understanding or semantic distance between two parties who speak different languages or belong to different cultures. ... In a good dialogue or conversation one listens to what the other says and tries to work out what they mean, tries to understand, to make sense. ... The idea is that dialogue moves forward to a consensus (of sorts). (Shanks and Hodder 1995: 6)

This mitigated consensus is the "fusion of horizons" of hermeneutics.

But the goal that Bakhtin endorses is not a consensus of any sort, no matter how careful it might be to maintain two irreducible viewpoints, because the removal of propositions from a speaker's position removes them from their unrepeatable context.

> The dialogic sense of truth manifests unfinalizability by existing on the "threshold" (*porog*) of several interacting consciousnesses, a "plurality" of "unmerged voices". Crucial here is the modifier *unmerged*. These voices cannot be contained within a single consciousness, as in monologism: rather, their separateness is essential to the dialogue. Even when they agree, as they may, they do so from different perspectives,

and different senses of the world. (Morson and Emerson 1990: 236–7, italics in original)

The "unmerged voices" of the total speech context are in conversation, and because of this they continue to represent situated positions, voices of speakers, instead of disembodied positions that inevitably slide into totalizing assertions (Bakhtin 1984: 93; Morson and Emerson 1990: 160).

Bakhtin's concept of the total context of communication engages the thorny issue of evaluation that has dogged interpretive archaeology since its introduction. We know that not all interpretations are equally good; how do we justify assuming the authority to advocate for some interpretations and against others (compare Shanks and Hodder 1995: 18–23, Shanks and Tilley 1987: 20–1)? For Bakhtin (1993), the requirement to evaluate words (and actions) is a moral imperative which cannot be evaded. In his view, communication matters, it has serious consequences, it shapes ongoing social reality (Bakhtin 1986: 119–20). These aspects of his arguments resonate with recent claims that archaeological discourse must be taken seriously because of its social consequences.

Accounts of the past created by archaeologists are utterances, social acts of communication oriented toward an addressee whose evaluation of the utterance is crucial to its realization as a meaningful action. Bakhtin (1986: 126) suggests that each speaker has in mind a particular response, or better, that speakers create their utterances for an ideal super-addressee: "Every dialogue takes place against the background of the responsive understanding of an invisibly present third party who stands above all the participants in the dialogue." The super-addressee, unlike the real participants in dialogue, can be counted on to understand and fairly judge the speaker. As Morson and Emerson (1990: 135) note, the realism of Bakhtin's view of the context of communication contrasts Bakhtin's account with the "undistorted and uncoerced communication" required by Habermas. Undistorted communication may be an ideal, realized only in the notion of the perfect listener. Bakhtin offers as examples of the super-addressee God, absolute truth, and science; in other words, abstract principles judging the value of the utterance.

Because every act of communication is meaningful only to the extent that it draws a response, if not from proximate participants in dialogue, from the super-addressee, the entire form of communication is shaped by assumptions about evaluation. The style adopted in writing is shaped by the context of communication. "The internal politics of style (how the elements are put together) is determined by its external politics" (Bakhtin 1981: 284). Thus "archaeological poetics" (Shanks and Hodder 1995: 28, Tilley 1993a) is concerned not only with the form of archaeological utterances but is intimately related to their claims to evaluation. The rhetoric of archaeological works presumes particular standards of evaluation of their truthfulness.

From this point of view, archaeologists who construct their accounts of the past with an eye toward the conventions of normal science are oriented toward a super-addressee whose positive judgment they value above all others. The shape of their discourse is conditioned by prior acts of communication through which they have come to understand and value positively the language of Science. Use of features of this language in their writing solicits a positive evaluation affirming success in communication. Archaeologists who conceive of their super-addressee differently can employ very different kinds of language, again in anticipation of a particular response. Rather than representing distortion in communication, the choices of language conditioned by the super-addressee are a necessary part of the total context of communication. They are what Bakhtin (1984: 195) calls a "sideways glance" toward the audience, acknowledging that effective communication is social.

The image of the super-addressee shapes the choices made among the available languages that a speaker could use. But speakers engage in dialogue with more prosaic addressees who potentially or actually respond with their own words and actions, embodying their evaluation of the original utterance. Science is represented in actual communication by particular individuals, as are other potential super-addressees. The actual evaluation of communicative acts in archaeology is widely marked, both formally and informally.

Citation of published works is an overt form of revoicing, through which new texts engage in dialogue with previous works. Citation studies in archaeology highlight the way citations shape the construction of knowledge. An early study explicitly argued that new research agendas could be seen emerging through citation practices during the period when critiques of culture-historical work gave way to the "New Archaeology" of the 1960s and 1970s in the United States (Sterud 1978). Pioneering analyses by feminist historical archaeologists documented patterns of gender differentiation in archaeological citations, both in the practices of citation by men and women, and in practices of citation of work by men and women (Beaudry and White 1994, Victor and Beaudry 1992). Women, as authors, cited significantly more sources than men did. At the same time, women's publications were less commonly cited, by men and women alike. Beaudry and White (1994: 155–8) dispelled what might have been the easiest explanation for the patterns they observed, simple bias against women as authors. Instead, they pointed to a more complex phenomenon in which women submitted fewer works for review. Their content analysis of citations demonstrated that women were most likely to write materials analysis papers. As Beaudry and White (1994: 156) note, these are not the kind of theoretical works that are cited repeatedly. What is revoiced in archaeological citation as it currently stands are general propositions, sweeping claims, and important statements, often about the origins of things.

These studies show, not surprisingly, that citation is never neutral. It always implies or specifies a judgment, engaging a previous source to reject or affirm it. Cited sources are "reaccentuated" in ways that transform the original statement into a trace of both their previous and their new contexts, binding contexts together through time (Bakhtin 1986: 89). As the reaccenting of prior speech creates an ongoing context through time (in this case, the discipline of archaeology), it simultaneously, dialogically, gives rise to a situated speaker engaged in that discipline. "Our own discourse is gradually and slowly wrought out of others' words that have been acknowledged and assimilated, and the boundaries between the two are at first scarcely perceptible" (Bakhtin 1981: 345). Reaccentuation and assimilation engage us in responding to and affirming authoritative and persuasive discourse through our revoicing of already spoken words.

Citation is simply one example of the overt forms of dialogic practice that underwrite the creation of the discipline as an ongoing conversation. Other examples include reviews, comments, and other formal exchanges. The evaluation of particular utterances through their incorporation in ongoing dialogue is more pervasive than the marked examples of these formal genres. Language, including newly coined terms and specific turns of phrase, enters into circulation and becomes so deeply embedded that it becomes unusual to cite a specific original speaker. Thus, in early archaeological texts, the language of a military campaign was adopted, sometimes self-consciously, because the writers found the narratives of hierarchical organization and order that it embodied persuasive. We foregrounded some highly self-conscious examples of the current affirmation and reaccentuation of this language in more recent texts. But the echoes of their revoicing live on throughout archaeological speech, largely as uninterrogated parts of our everyday practices. Every trench that we excavate owes something to the language of war.

The echoes of the original speakers, or writers, live on and inhabit texts that revoice their words. Words bind together the participants in the ongoing dialogues through which we produce knowledge. The circulation of revoiced words delimits archaeologists as participants in a dialogue in a specific place and time. The way we imagine our standpoints in time and space is germane to any attempts we might want to make to create new forms of writing.

Speaking from a Particular Place and Time: Chronotopes and Genres

Central to the total context of communication are the temporal and spatial relations between a writer or speaker and the subjects about whom and to whom she is speaking, embodied in Bakhtin's concept of the chronotope (Bakhtin 1981: 84–258, 1986: 10–59). Chronotopes are what give coherence to particular genres. They are the way that a specific representation portrays space–time. "Bakhtin's crucial point is that time and space vary in *qualities*: different social activities and representations of those activities presume different kinds of time and space" (Morson and Emerson 1990: 367). The ways that archaeologists write about our own experiences and about those of other people in the past are grounded in chronotopes that, like the language we use, are historical and dialogic. The shift in emphasis between the regional scope and long-term temporality of evolutionary explanations, and the insistently local and day-to-day temporality of household archaeology (Tringham 1991: 119–24, 2000: 121–6), exemplifies two different archaeological chronotopes. We write in the chronotopes we receive from the past and reaccent them as we write. The reason that choosing a form in which to write matters is that choosing a genre is a choice also of a chronotope, and thus of what Bakhtin (1984: 96–8, 110) calls a "form-shaping ideology."

This is better shown than said. It is possible to suggest that archaeology has exploited two chronotopes extensively. One of these is evolution (or progress), the other discovery (or experience). The chronotope of progress is clearly ideological (Johnson 1999: 132–47, Pluciennik 1999: 661, Shanks and Tilley 1987: 53–6). It transforms sequence in time into a chain of cause and effect with an underlying directionality toward complexity or improvement. What may be less obvious, because it is so fundamental, is that progress implies a particular kind of space–time context. Because events are subordinated to a long-term directionality, the chronotope of progress takes place at the macroscale. It deals in regions and epochs, in cultures or societies. The fine-grain of the everyday is irrelevant, or worse: it is distracting, introducing too much noise. Individual action or performance is predetermined and agency is simply not a question. The relationship of the writer to the events he describes is fixed as retrospective and removed: the chronotope of progress has already happened and the writer is positioned on its periphery.

In the chronotope of discovery, the writer is positioned inside, even at the center, of things. Like progress, discovery is ideological (Shanks and Tilley 1987: 86–90). " 'Discovery' is fascinating. It is part of the romance of archaeology. 'Discovery' links past and present, reaching out from incessant passing of the momentary present, bringing the chasm between past and present opened up by the conception of time as an empty spatial dimension filled with artifacts locked into their respective presents" (Shanks and Tilley 1987: 71). The time and space of discovery is a kind of *now*, from which the writer reports directly observed facts. Actions over time are subordinated to the timeless moment, a moment in which the significance of things is pinned down.

As chronotopes, progress and discovery shape archaeological writing. Differences between chronotopes lie in the way that time and space, cause and their effect, are represented.

> The chronotope makes narrative events concrete, makes them take on flesh, causes blood to flow in their veins . . . the chronotope provides the ground essential for the showing-forth, the representability of events. And this is so thanks precisely to the special increase in density and concreteness of time markers – the time of human life, of historical time – that occurs within well-delineated spatial areas. (Bakhtin 1981: 250)

The flesh on the bones of progress and discovery is relatively thin. Discovery bears close comparison to adventure time, one of the chronotopes defined by Bakhtin (1981: 89–102), typified by popular culture (including *Raiders of the Lost Ark* and its stereotypic archaeologist Indiana Jones) that "does not seem to be especially productive of new insights about the nature of actions and events" (Morson and Emerson 1990: 371–2). Progress is a form of eschatology, a utopian chronotope in which the "separating segment of time loses its significance and interest, it is merely an unnecessary continuation of an indefinitely prolonged present," an impediment in the inevitable move to a more highly valued end of time (Bakhtin 1981: 148).

Archaeological writing develops specific chronotopes over time in generic narratives, examples of which will be explored throughout succeeding chapters. Path-breaking discussions of narrative in archaeology (Hodder 1995, Landau 1991, Pluciennik 1999, Terrell 1990) have been grounded in Hayden White's (1973, 1978, 1987) analyses of historical narratives, and Vladimir Propp's (1968) analysis of folkloric narrative. These discussions take as defining features of narratives a sequential plot that gives coherent meaning to events that occur to characters. Different "narrative forms" employ distinct rhetorical tropes and advance different ideologies (White 1973).

Hodder (1995) applies White's schema to an analysis of his own writing about change over time in the south Scandinavian Neolithic, exploring the applicability of White's proposed sequence of tropes to shifts in material culture and the narratives he created to give shape to it. As he notes, both the specific idea of an inherent cycle of tropes, and the proposed dominance of single tropes, are questionable aspects of White's essentially structural approach (see also Hodder 1993). Pluciennik (1999: 662) underlines the same conclusion, commenting that "the degree of overlap and lack of agreement with White's categories suggests that this approach is not necessarily the most fruitful" for the analysis of archaeological narratives.

White's "narrative forms" come close to Bakhtin's concept of genres as "form-shaping ideologies," but they differ in a crucial way. Where White's narrative forms are essentially static and classificatory, genres are emergent and active.

> Genres convey a vision of the world not by explicating a set of propositions but by developing concrete examples . . . they allow the reader to view the world in a specific way. A particular sense of experience, never formalized, guides the author's efforts in creating his or her work. Each author who contributes to the genre learns to experience the world in the genre's way. (Morson and Emerson 1990: 282)

The active nature of Bakhtin's concept of genre equally distinguishes it from the Formalist approach to narrative (Morson and Emerson 1990: 18–19, 272–5). Formalist analysis treated literary works as construction problems, in which literary devices, including characters, were employed to bind together various linguistic segments of which a text was composed. From this perspective "genre is a specific way of deploying a hierarchy of devices" (Morson and Emerson 1990: 273). That Propp's (1968) study of folk tales can be used productively in the analysis of narratives of the past, as it has been (Landau 1991, Terrell 1990), is an indictment of the mechanistic and impoverished nature of writing about the past.

As Pluciennik (1999: 667) notes, the majority of archaeological narratives "present not only a characteristic narrative chronological position and tense – that of hindsight offered as a sequential story of, rather than in, the past – but also a markedly external or bird's-eye view. The story is typically told in the third-person passive, giving an often spurious sense of objective description," less commonly

> in the (authorial) first person, which at least emphasizes the intervention, constructed interpretation, and manipulation of the material by the writer. There is usually little sense of actions, events, or history considered from the actor's point of view ... if there is a rhetoric of empathy, it is with the intellectual (and less often emotional) journey and experience of the author rather than of any past Others, who are represented in a distanced manner.

The one deletion in the preceding quote is a reference to experimental archaeological writing that Pluciennik exempts from this blanket characterization.

These experiments, I suggest, have had the same effect within archaeological writing that novels, in Bakhtin's view, had on narrative fiction. The novel

> takes as its special concern the ways in which various languages of heteroglossia may enter into dialogue with each other and the kinds of complex interactions that such dialogues produce. . . . When languages enter into dialogue, complex changes take place. . . . To begin with, a language that has entered into dialogue with another language, especially if that dialogue concerns the topic or experience to which the language is specially adapted, loses its "naivete". It becomes self-conscious, because it has seen itself from an alien perspective and has come to understand how its own values and beliefs appear to the other language. When it is used subsequently, such a language can no longer directly and unself-consciously talk about its topic as if there were no other plausible way of doing so. (Morson and Emerson 1990: 309)

In the same way, archaeological narratives written self-consciously become novelized (Morson and Emerson 1990: 304); they take into account their own contingency and the real possibility of other ways of telling the story. One of the major changes in contemporary archaeology is that new genres embodying different chronotopes are being created, sites for new dialogue between archaeologists and nonarchaeologists.

3

Dialogues Heard and Unheard, Seen and Unseen

Second Dialogue: *"This Is the Center of Their Own World": Making Sense of Mantecales*

It's a Friday morning in December, and while I am never happy to be expected to think at nine in the morning, I am delighted on this occasion: the long-awaited oral exam to admit Jeanne Lopiparo (see chapter 4) to admission for candidacy for the Ph.D. (As she will inform me later that afternoon, at Berkeley there is actually a degree that someone who never advances beyond this stage receives, the Candidate in Philosophy degree, but even without that, I have come to think that this is really the pivotal moment for anyone in a Ph.D. program. It is the first, and at Berkeley the last, time that the candidate will meet with the dissertation committee for a sustained examination of the shape of the thesis project. It is our most real rite of passage; at the end of the examination, the candidate is accepted as a beginning peer.)

So I cannot excuse my inattention somewhere over two hours later, on the basis of the sleepiness of a natural night person, or by a lack of interest in the candidate, the subject, or the occasion. But for a matter of several minutes I simply am not in the room in Berkeley. Instead, I am torn away and taken back to Honduras, in the summer of 1995, when five advanced students struggled to understand something truly unintelligible at a site called Mantecales, on an abandoned course of the Río Chamelecon, today occupied by the last trickles of the Quebrada Chasnigua.

"This is the center of their own world": the words, the voice, the situated speaking position are those of Ruth Tringham. She is urging, coaxing, perhaps simply inviting Jeanne to follow her own inclination, to describe her dissertation project in terms of its own space and time in hamlets of the Ulúa River Valley around AD 850.

But the words could stand as well as the epigraph for Operation 4 at Mantecales.

Before we ever began our field season, we had hints that our Honduran colleagues had recovered something unusual at this site: our first *in situ* marble artifact. Despite our intensive research over the preceding fifteen years, we had never recovered even a fragment of one of the elaborately carved marble vases, the primary luxury item for which the Ulúa Valley is known. The Mantecales marble vase fragment was unusual: green, rather than clear white, and lacking the diagnostic carved scrolls of the Ulúa marble vases. But it suggested a unique potential for understanding how these objects were used. Even though it was a fragment, a base lacking most of the rim, it had been recovered in a context that was either a unique structured deposit or a very intense and selective midden. Our Honduran colleagues lacked the resources to continue excavations at Mantecales, which they had conducted in advance of construction that would destroy the site. As is typical of our role in the management of the archaeological sites in the region, we were invited to devote some of our efforts to adding to knowledge of this piece of Honduras' cultural heritage.

The five students returning as volunteers would, we decided, have the opportunity to work at Mantecales, at least long enough to clarify for us what the context of this marble vessel had been. Each of these students had already worked with us on other sites, had learned the system of excavating and recording that we employed, and knew the basic framework we were exploring for the valley. Each of them brought their own interests and experiences as well, ranging from faunal and lithic analysis to the exploration of ritual spaces and community identity. Because our primary commitment was to continued work at another site, the Mantecales crew would be working largely independently, but we did not anticipate that any complex or difficult decisions would come up that they could not handle. In fifteen years of excavations, the last five directed exclusively at similar sites, low *lomas* – earthen "tells" – in the central floodplain, we had developed a fairly good idea of what to expect, and these students had been exposed to everything we knew about excavating *lomas*.

Which was a very good thing, because that way, they were able to recognize that nothing was proceeding as expected. Not that the technical tasks of identifying loci, describing and mapping them, and removing them, were particularly difficult. But despite being able to identify soil features, the Mantecales crew were not identifying features like any they had seen before in their prior excavations. They rapidly outlined the surface our Honduran colleagues told us had supported dense ceramic lenses, covering the fragment of a green marble vase. Moving below that surface, they outlined a small rectangular chamber formed by cobblestone wall lines.

Stone is not common in the *lomas*, located as they are on flood-plain deposits, but the excavators had seen other stone features before, and the system we use makes it relatively easy to label and map stone features without worrying too much about what they mean. Still, when I came out to the site on my next rounds, we had some discussion of other small chambers that I had worked on, at Cerro Palenque and Travesía. Just keep working, I told them; it will clarify itself. Be sure to separate deposits from the different sides of the walls, and watch for the surfaces on which the walls were built. Remember, things don't float in midair, so even if you can't see a contrast, when you reach the bottom of the rocks, you are at a surface. And don't forget that the inside and outside surfaces don't need to line up; remember remodelling. Split things as much as you need now; we can always lump later, but it is usually not possible to split in the lab.

And I went away, interested that they had a stone structure, but not particularly worried about it. So perhaps I deserved the surprise that came that afternoon, when instead of returning from the field, the Mantecales crew sent an urgent message: there was something they couldn't leave out overnight. Of course, we went back to the site. And there they were, with the stone cist outlined and its contents partly exposed, including a number of articulated ceramic vessels, some of them in the form of effigies. I must admit that my memory elides them all, but that doesn't matter, because as they worked, they had begun to create an exquisitely detailed set of drawings. These reveal layer after layer of smashed vessels, mixed in with carbon and a meager amount of soil. The effigy incense-burners were the most spectacular, and created our greatest dilemmas. We consulted with the conservators at the local museum on how to excavate them to minimize damage and make reconstruction easier. Eventually, the two jaguar effigies and a one-third life-size human figure were carried to the museum, where months later we were able to photograph the restored vessels.

Clearly, this was not a small storage room adjacent to a household group, like those at Cerro Palenque. Our question about whether the marble vessel fragment was simply discarded in a midden, or part of a structured deposit, would seem to have been answered as well: the marble sherd was placed on a surface capping the cobble chamber, and in turn covered by dense deposits of smashed pottery. The field crew asked a reasonable question: What was this? I responded by explaining the concept of structured deposition, and luckily, they didn't notice that it wasn't an answer in the terms their question actually required. How, after all, could I answer the question, "What does this signify?" when we had never found anything even remotely like this before?

Obviously, by casting my net a little wider. In the Ulúa Valley, we had recovered effigy censers before, although always discarded, in fragments, in midden or reused in fill. We also had recovered individual examples of many of the other vessels present in the deposit, including the small, unslipped cup-shaped pots called *candaleros*. While some people argued that these were paint pots, the context at Mantecales matched our other good contexts, in which they seemed to be used for burning something.

As I would later find by doing a simple statistical test of association, at Puerto Escondido, the other site we were simultaneously excavating, *candaleros* tended to be found near burials significantly more often than would be expected by chance. While in the field, I reacted from a general impression of such an association, and began to think about the possibility that the Mantecales deposit covered a burial.

Nothing like this has been found in the Ulúa Valley, but at the contemporary Classic Maya monumental center, Copan, three hours' drive to the west, multiple figural censer lids were recovered on top of the stone chamber of a burial located in a pyramid. The cobble chamber in the low earthen *loma* at Mantecales was clearly not the same kind of context as the cut-stone burial vault in the pyramid at Copan. Nor was our concept of the social life of the Ulúa Valley at all commensurate with the centralized hierarchy at Copan. Still, I decided that it might be worthwhile mentioning the possibility to the excavators. They should be watching for any sign of a burial.

This, I think, seemed to the crew a more intelligible description of the context than the more neutral "structured deposition" I had initially offered. It gave them something to watch out for. But virtually as soon as I had uttered this argument, Mantecales offered its next word in the dialogue. Centered in the chamber, the unbroken rim of a large jar was traced out. Smashed pottery, obsidian artifacts, and the carbon-rich dirt was present both inside the limits of the pot rim, and outside them. Perhaps the burial was secondary, or juvenile, placed in the vessel, as some Nicaraguan pots I knew from the Peabody Museum had been used. Nicaragua, with its less stratified societies, was a much better analogy than Copan, given the social models we espouse for the Ulúa Valley.

As the rim was cleared, I was even able to identify the pottery type for the excavators. I don't know how reassuring they found this, but for me, it was a return to intelligibility: if there is one thing I can do when all else fails, it is to identify where in the highly complex pottery taxonomies of the valley a vessel belongs. One of the disturbing things about the figural censers, for me, was that they are so unusual that I really worry about our understanding of when they were made. I know that at least one large-scale human effigy was discarded in the late days of Cerro Palenque, probably after AD 1000. The examples from the tomb at Copan were much earlier, and occasional fragments in contexts in the Ulúa Valley suggested they were made throughout the period of manufacture of Ulúa Polychrome ceramics, from about AD 500 to 850.

The jar whose rim we located belonged to the later part of that Classic period of polychrome manufacture. This made sense, because the polychrome vases mixed in the deposit were of the Santana type, notable for its black backgrounds and elaborate figural scenes, a type I assign to about AD 750–850. Everything was fine, in fact: the deposit of ceramics that capped the marble vessel sherd entirely lacked polychromes, instead being dominated by unslipped fine-paste pottery typical during the Terminal Classic (ca. 850–1050 AD).

We could begin to see these contexts as evidence of repeated action. This began with a burial, yet to be uncovered, in the base of the stone chamber. Either as part of funeral rites or later commemorative actions, multiple incense burners were employed, smashed and thrown into the chamber with their contents.

(Incense-burning ceremonies are among the best documented ritual actions in all of Classic Maya studies, and the texts describing these actions are well understood. One of the standard images of Classic Maya Piedras Negras, a site located on the border of Mexico and Guatemala, shows the ruler holding a hanging bag. These bags have been identified as incense bags for a very long time, primarily by comparison with incense bags in use in the sixteenth-century Aztec capital, Tenochtitlan. The human-effigy censer lid from Mantecales showed a standing male figure, holding out one hand. Separately in the deposit, we recovered a ceramic effigy of an incense bag, in the same paste and style of execution. Two holes pierced in the upper margin would have allowed the bag to hang from a perishable cord looped over the outstretched hand of the human figure, who thus became a reflexive image: both an incense-burning vessel and an incense-burning person.)

Then, perhaps not very long after the funerary or commemorative ritual, use of the area was terminated in an event, perhaps a feast, marked by the use and breaking of large numbers of fine serving vessels and the disposal of at least one fine carved stone vase. The time elapsed could have been as much as 300 years, but equally, and more likely, could have been much shorter, covering the documented transition from the manufacture of late Santana polychromes to early fine-paste vessels, a matter of potters over a single generation living around AD 850.

Thinking in terms of generations soon became urgently necessary, because when the excavators arrived at the base of the jar neck, they found that it was set inside a second jar neck, and that one, in turn, was set in a third. And while the second jar neck could have been contemporaneous with the uppermost, the third was something else again. It was of a type normally associated with slightly earlier Ulúa polychromes of the Travesía group. With a feeling of total disorientation I checked the contents from the contexts around the third jar neck, and indeed, found that the associated polychromes had changed.

Or actually, of course, had not changed. What changed was our perspective, and I had to rapidly think things through again. No human remains, other than a couple of loose teeth, had been found in the course of excavating the chamber to the depth of the three jar rims. Incense-burning vessels formed part of the contexts all the way down the base of the chamber. Clearly, the incense burning could not be funerary. Commemoration seemed a likelier alternative, with incense burning taking place over at least a couple of generations, perhaps spanning the period of transition from the manufacture of Travesía polychromes to Santana polychromes, around AD 750. The capping of the area a century later, while reflecting knowledge of the previous use of the area, was discontinuous with the earlier commemorative actions (there was, after all, a surface under the marble vase). The stack of jar rims might have served as a central conduit for offerings, a metaphorical connection between the buried deposits and the later people who considered them significant enough to mark over time.

It still seemed most likely that the stack of rims connected a burial of someone who had come to be considered an important ancestor by those who maintained access to the grave. So I urged the excavators to continue their careful work excavating the deposit. But I began to hedge my bets, and returned to structured deposition – even if we did not uncover a burial, we were for certain in the presence of highly structured deposition. I reminded the crew (and myself!) that burials in the valley generally don't seem to be elaborated as are those of Maya sites in the west and north. Instead of a human burial, perhaps we could look forward to finding a whole feline skeleton, laid out and covered in red pigment, something that had been reported from a nearby site in the valley, in Doris Stone's excavations at Travesía.

I was briefly comforted when the stone walls of the chamber ended, at the level of the bottom of the third jar neck. But just as quickly, this comfort turned inside out: the third jar neck rested in yet another jar rim. In all, four more jar necks, for a total of seven, made up the stack. The lower four appeared to have been placed during a single period, when earlier Ulúa polychromes, the Santa Rita group, were in use, a period I had previously estimated dated to around AD 550–650. If I wanted evidence of commemorative activities showing maintenance of memory of place over a long period, now I had it; at a minimum, the deposits around the stack of jar rims covered a period of over 100 years. And if this was somehow a commemoration of a buried ancestor, the burial of that individual still lay further down.

And so, apologetically, I asked the crew to continue. In a separate excavation begun by our Honduran colleagues, the base of the *loma* had been reached; surely, if we continued excavation to that level, something would be clarified. Either we would locate a burial, or the nature of the deposits would settle down into something that fit into our range of known *loma* features.

Mantecales did not like to be taken for granted. The excavators continued down, now through extensive area-wide deposits of alternating dense carbon and fine, sandy clay soil. The striped appearance that these deposits made was like a parody of stratigraphy, but there were no features within the excavated two-by-two-meter blocks to clarify the formation of these layers. Finally, they ended, and a dense clay was all that was left to the depth of the base of the *loma*. As I reassured the field crew, at least we knew that the pattern of burning and dumping that characterized the later levels also characterized the earlier ones. And while we hadn't uncovered a burial, after all, we had to expect that, in the Ulúa Valley, with its emphasis on corporate houses instead of unique individuals, special places were less likely to be personalized. The continued use of the *loma* over multiple generations would have been a powerful way for a social group to form and re-form its identity. And I tried not to say to them what I said to my codirector: "What if there is a burial, offset from this location? Short of bringing in a backhoe, how could we ever hope to find it?"

"Double-Voiced Narration": Retelling
Archaeological Narratives

Looking back now, with Ruth Tringham's words echoing in my ears, I realize that I was concerned with the wrong thing. Ruth was commenting on the master narrative that she notes dominates the way that those of us working in Honduras frame our research, however much we try to escape it. This is the view from the west, from the Classic Maya sites, toward the "periphery" of their world, the Ulúa Valley. The official designation of the area as the periphery of Mesoamerica or of the Maya world is reflected in multiple articles, and most maps and textbooks. As I like to say, since the area immediately east and south is sometimes called the "Intermediate Area" – intermediate between Mesoamerican and Andean civilizations – the Ulúa Valley could be best described as the northern periphery of the Intermediate Area. This is part of what Payson Sheets (1992) characterized as the problem of the "pervasive pejorative" in studies of lower Central America: a definition by lack.

I have often written and lectured in opposition to the framing of the valley in this way (R. Joyce 1991, 1992c, 1993a, 1996b). Acting as archaeological curators for a museum in San Pedro Sula, Honduras, my codirector and I made sure that the maps showing interaction were centered on the valley and included links in all directions. We count as one of our great achievements the publication of an article in the popular journal, *New Scientist* (Daviss 1997) that accepted the alternative narrative we supplied, in which the Ulúa Valley was worth studying because nothing unusual happened there. The article quotes us saying things like "Orthodoxy in the past, and still to some degree, says that if Honduran people weren't doing proper hieroglyphic inscriptions and other standard classic Mayan stuff, then they were howling barbarians who were trying to be Mayas and failing," "Some people were wealthier, but the difference from humble homes to elaborate ones is more gradual – and there's a complete lack of the grand palaces we see at Mayan sites" and "People sometimes understood that greater stratification isn't necessarily good. If you're the aristocrat king wannabe, you have a very different perspective from the guy who would have to grow an extra corn crop to pay for your palace" (Daviss 1997: 39, 41).

In our developing view of the area, we talk about unusual sites like Mantecales as the homesteads of groups of "wealthy farmers." But despite all of this, when it came to the practical day-to-day guidance of the excavations at Mantecales, I drew freely, and misleadingly, from the conceptual vocabulary of the archaeology of centralized Maya states. Copan in particular, where I looked for my guiding analogy, is a site I have strenuously argued – against considerable resistance – had little direct or even mediated contact with settlements in the Ulúa Valley (R. Joyce 1988, 1991: 135–9, 1993a). While I was actively engaged in dialogue on this point with my colleagues in the field, that dialogue was less influential on me than the presence of a super-addressee whose response I was inherently seeking in the shaping of our field narratives. An unintelligible narrative would be far harder to make into a text, and indeed, the story of Mantecales has yet to see a formal publication, even though I think we have arrived at quite a good understanding of the context (including other excavations not described in this narrative).

This shaping of our understanding, of the story line that gives not only coherence (Hodder 1999: 55–6) but *value* to the knowledge we construct, is a crucial part of the narrativization of research that goes on as we engage in it. We shape our understanding in dialogue with the already existing world of words that come to us already inflected by their use in other contexts. In my story about our work at Mantecales, in fact, a major part of the shaping of the narrative came through the use of a few specific terms. Two of these are widely employed in Central American archaeology, and engaged us in narratives from wider domains. The third is a neologism, a word my codirector and I made up specifically to escape a narrative that did not work. Considering the work those words do should help illuminate why I suggest that the concept of revoicing is crucial to understanding our disciplinary production of knowledge: "retelling a text in one's own words is to a certain extent a double-voiced narration of another's words" (Bakhtin 1981: 341).

The three words that carry forward the narrative of Mantecales, and that shaped it in the field, are *incensario, candalero,* and *loma.* All three are Spanish words used in archaeological English in the area, a familiar aspect of the regionalization of archaeology. The use of words borrowed from another language echoes two different languages; it is, in Bakhtin's terms, heteroglossia. Their use echoes the contexts in which the words are used in a nonspecialized way, something that has been critiqued as a source of unreflective and misleading interpretation in archaeology (Allison 1999). At the same time, the words echo very specific histories of use within a strand of archaeological discourse.

In Christopher Tilley's (1999: 82–95) exploration of the genealogy of "megalith," a similarly pervasive word that immediately demarcates an archaeological dialect and narrative dialogues, he draws attention to the way that the term persists despite being resignified. Fotiadis (1992: 138–44) explored the disciplinary coding of the similarly persistent, and more universal, word-concept "site." Hamilton (2000) has characterized the history-laden nature of terms used by archaeologists as a "conceptual archive." Bakhtin draws attention to the fact that, more than simply structuring our questions and answers, using already voiced words embodies an engagement with others. By telling the story in someone else's words, I respond to someone else's narrative and appeal for evaluation within the context of that narrative.

An *incensario* is any vessel that an archaeologist thinks was used in the process of burning incense. In the Maya area, *incensarios* include a wide range of forms, most of which have little contextual evidence of use in ritual. One form of *incensario* includes vessels with evidence of burning, while another comprises elaborately modeled forms. In Honduras, burned *incensarios* are most often found with cooking refuse (Hendon 1991, R. Joyce 1991: 103, 108–9, 113, Urban and Smith 1987). Effigy figures and other modeled forms on lids have distinctive distributions, but they commonly lack evidence of burning. It appears most likely that there were vessels made to be used to contain fire (braziers), whether that fire was to be used for cooking, heating, or as the site for depositing resin to produce scented smoke. When the latter activity was involved, in some times and places, a lid with a modeled effigy was placed on top of the brazier, usually with tubes and holes arranged so that smoke would stream out of the body of the animal or person in visually arresting ways.

At Mantecales, the distinctive ceramic censers we found were effigy figures on lids. We also recovered other forms, such as "frying-pan" or ladle censers, shallow bowls with pierced bases, attached to a tubular handle, showing evidence of burning in the interior bowl base. And of course, these vessels were deposited intermixed with carbon. Calling them *incensarios* did not seem in any way premature, and the interpretation of the vessels as used in specialized burning of resins seems quite strong. But using the word did engage us in the narrative where it has already been accentuated and given meaning, in the archaeology of the Classic Maya. It brought with it a series of expectations, most of which were disappointed.

The second heteroglossic term used in the Mantecales narrative, *candalero*, demonstrates more clearly why engaging with existing narratives, revoicing existing words, might be a problem. *Candaleros*, originally named for their resemblance to contemporary candle-holders, are normally small, single tubular ceramic vessels. They tend to be poorly finished, although some have incised or punctate decoration. In the Ulúa Valley, they are often friable, suggesting either a very coarse clay mixture or low firing temperature, or both. Since they were identified, debate has centered on what they were used for: did they (like modern candle-holders) support some sort of light source, perhaps pitch-pine torches? Or were they paint pots, or containers for other small-volume liquids? Were they a sort of personal incense burner? Distributions of *candaleros* are closest to those of braziers, and they are found both in household and non-residential contexts. But even in household contexts, they may have been used in domestic ritual.

The Mantecales contexts, and the impetus they provided for the statistical test of association between *candaleros* and burials at Puerto Escondido, would seem to provide support for the interpretation of *candaleros* as personal censers. But this entire set of questions were framed by the initial naming of the vessel form as a *candalero*. Many other questions that surround the manufacture and use of these small vessels are pushed to one side by the dialogic narrative that has unfolded since they were first named as a subject of archaeological inquiry. To take one example: similar small vessel forms are found throughout northern Honduras during the Classic period, but otherwise, they appear to be made only at the contemporaneous Mexican city, Teotihuacan, far to the west. This might seem like a completely accidental resemblance with no significance. But other artifact and architectural details, and obsidian traded from Central Mexican sources, suggest that there was some kind of poorly understood contact between these widely separated regions that simply does not form part of accepted archaeological narratives. And so Honduran *candaleros* are narrativized strictly in terms of their function, rather than as words in a dialogue about long-distance connections.

The third Spanish loan word I used in talking about Mantecales, *loma*, is as foreign to other archaeologists specializing in Honduras and Central America as to those working elsewhere. The word refers to a low rise on the landscape. It is borrowed from the common terminology for landforms in Honduras, where it is one of a series of words used with no cultural interpretive intention. In our narratives, it replaces another word from local Spanish, *monticulo*, which translates in English as "mound." In the English used by New World archaeologists, a mound is a heavily accentuated word. It is the term used since the eighteenth century for the landforms that, on excavation, proved to contain Native American burials and caches, or the remains of pyramids supporting temples. As *monticulos*, the landforms we are excavating could only be compared to Maya pyramids.

And those comparisons were always disadvantageous: no *loma* is as tall as the tallest Maya pyramid mounds. Those comparisons also failed to capture what most interests us about the *lomas*: that they were built up over generations through a sequence of remodelling of groups of buildings, some of which are superimposed, others displaced, in the fashion of the spectrum Ruth Tringham (2000) outlines for Near Eastern tells.

We introduced the word *loma* in order to escape the constraints of the narratives incorporated in "mounds." Had we taken the leap of using the word "tell," we would have connected our discussion to the narratives that in fact seem most pertinent to us. But here we must remember that the total context of a dialogue is shaped by the speaker's ideas about the listener.

> The speaker strives to get a reading on his own word, and on his own conceptual horizon, that determines this word, within the alien horizon of the understanding receiver; he enters into dialogical relationships with certain aspects of this horizon. The speaker breaks through the alien horizon of the listener, constructs his utterance on alien territory against his, the listener's, apperceptive background (Bakhtin 1981: 282)

The narrative is dialogic; it reaches out for evaluation towards a specific addressee and superaddressee. We did not adopt the term "tell" because we were concerned to engage archaeologists for whom the expected English word is "mound."

We write very differently depending on the audience we imagine. The effect of the imagined audience is usefully represented by genres, and by subgenres. The generic expectations towards which archaeologists address their writing suggest that genres embody notional super-addressees. In archaeology, super-addresses and their genres most clearly take the form of specific journals, with their own heteroglossic languages. When we write about our Honduran research for *Yaxkin*, the journal published in Spanish by the Honduran Institute of Anthropology and History, everything is different from the way the same material is presented for *Latin American Antiquity*. Compare the summaries of two articles presenting research related to that described in the *New Scientist* article quoted above:

> Rather than an isolated, backward rural village on the edge of the Mesoamerican world, the Middle Formative society of which Playa de los Muertos was part had a continuous history going back as early as any sedentary society yet documented in Mesoamerica. Like other precocious Mesoamerican societies, the people of the Chotepe phase Ulúa valley participated in long-distance networks of exchange through

which obsidian from Guatemala moved as far west as the Gulf Coast Olmec centers. . . . The participation of villages in far eastern Mesoamerica in these networks demands re-evaluation of core-periphery models of the development of Mesoamerican complex societies. . . . It is highly unlikely that Puerto Escondido is unique, and much more likely that the agricultural potential of lowland river valleys in Mesoamerica would have made them some of the most favorable locations – along with swamps and lacustrine environments – for early transitions to increased reliance on agriculture and to sedentism. . . . That other equally early villages exist elsewhere in eastern Mesoamerica seems certain. The identification of early settlements in areas of active river deposition may be difficult, but it is crucial to arriving at more accurate understandings of the early history of human occupation in Central America. (Joyce and Henderson 2001)

In summary, the excavations at Puerto Escondido provide evidence that the lower Ulúa River Valley was occupied more than a thousand years before the Playa phase of the Middle Formative. The inhabitants of the valley in this early time period worked intensively in obsidian, and worked less common materials – sea shell, marble, jade – in specialized craft production. Beginning at the start of the Early Formative Period, ceramics testify that the inhabitants of Puerto Escondido maintained continuous contact with communities in other parts of Mesoamerica. . . . Puerto Escondido demonstrates, for the first time, a sequence of continuous occupation from the end of the Archaic to the end of the Classic period. There are few sites in any part of Mesoamerica with such evidence of continuous occupation. No other site in Honduras has such rich evidence of the early epochs of the history of the country. (Henderson and Joyce in press; my translation)

The concepts and many of the words are the same. But for the Honduran audience of the latter article, which began as a public presentation, the local significance is more important; Puerto Escondido is a resource for the history (not prehistory) of the country. For the readers of Latin American Antiquity – a subset of the members of the Society for American Archaeology – the site is significant as a piece of evidence for wider issues of the transition to agriculture and specific processes of long-distance exchange. Such contrasts are most obvious when archaeologists engage others outside the discipline (see chapter 5). But even in intradisciplinary writing, the expectation of an evaluative response shapes archaeological narratives. Together, the horizon embodied in a specific chronotope and the super-addressee whose evaluative judgment is imagined shape archaeological writing into genres.

Muted Multivocality: The Monologic
Writing of Archaeology

The account I gave of the work at Mantecales at the beginning of this chapter differs from a more conventional version of events by fore-grounding the way that discussion of the emerging contexts in the field, among a cast of more than seven characters, shaped our under-standing, structured our excavations, and led to an understanding that was far from total. In this process, I responded not only to the speak-ers present on the site, but also to the past speakers whose words I knew through reading them in texts. And all of us, those present on site and present only in scraps of textual memory, engaged in dia-logues with others, including the past inhabitants of Mantecales whose material "utterances" continually contradicted me.

Narrativizing knowledge production in the texts we write is, from this perspective, simply a recovery of the multiple voices already in the work of archaeology. Ian Hodder (1989b) has explored the move away from overt narration in archaeological texts toward the domi-nant late-twentieth-century genre, the site report. He notes that many of the late-eighteenth-century reports he discusses were in the form of letters, often employing a description of discovery in what I would argue is a persistent archaeological chronotope. By the late nineteenth and early twentieth century, reports take the form of the segregation of findings into categories, and the first-person narrator is banished. Hodder (1989b) draws particular attention to the fact that, despite a move toward multiple authorship, late twentieth-century archaeolo-gical reports present conclusions without any of the actual debate and discussion that takes place among the multiple members of any archaeological project. He calls for a return of the narrator's voice, of the narration of a sequence of events, and the incorporation of more of the real dialogue among participants in the written text.

The arguments made in this short article are rich, and this summary cannot do justice to all of them. Some of these points are obviously in line with those discussed in previous chapters, and will be taken up again in the chapters that follow. Here, I want to focus on the nature of the changes in archaeological genres identified by Hodder, and extend his discussion from the conventional genres of the late twentieth century to the emerging body of experimental genres in archaeology that exemplify narrative and dialogue.

The use of letters, or extracts from letters, as the framework for late-eighteenth- and early-nineteenth-century archaeological reports recalls Bakhtin's discussion of epistolary novels. "A characteristic feature of the letter is an acute awareness of the interlocutor, the addressee to whom it is directed. The letter, like a rejoinder in a dialogue, is addressed to a specific person, and it takes into account the other's possible reactions, the other's possible reply" (Bakhtin 1984: 205). Letters are formed by expectations, so they are infused with double-voiced words, chosen "from two points of view simultaneously: as [the writer] himself understands them and wants others to understand them, and as another might actually understand them" (Bakhtin 1984: 208).

The move toward the conventional site report from the earlier epistolary genre might seem to be an abandonment of narration, an exclusion of dialogue. But either of these are impossible moves, given Bakhtin's insistence on dialogue as fundamental to all social acts of communication. The masking of narrative has been shown to have political causes, not only in archaeology but in science more generally. Rom Harré (1990) suggests that scientific reports in fact are narratives of a particular sort, in which the omission of the implied phrase "I know" before statements that are presented as facts is "a speech-act . . . effective in generating trust . . . because the speaker or writer is manifestly a member of an esoteric order, a 'community of saints' from membership in which the force of the claim descends" (Harré 1990: 82; compare Rose 1993: 205). The writer is implicitly saying "we" as a way of citing a community of faith in the production of truth through shared procedures. The omitted "I know" corresponds to a request: "trust me." Harré argues that this trust is founded on an assessment of reliability of other scientists for the core work of a science, which he identifies as including debate and specific forms of scientific practice. "One trusts that making use of a claim to know originated by one of one's fellow scientists will not let one down in a debate, and that making use of someone's claim to have successfully manipulated something will help to make one's own techniques and equipment work in practical contexts" (Harré 1990: 83).

Through the use of "we" by scientists, whether covertly implicit in passive constructions or actively employed, as is especially the case in speech, "a narrative structure is created within which the interlocutor is trapped" that "prevents that addressee taking up a hostile or rejecting stance to what has been said. Trust in the other is induced through the device of combining it with trust in oneself" (Harré 1990: 85). Harré's concern with the way that this form of narrative implicates entire disciplinary communities has obvious salience for archaeology. He notes that "to publish abroad a discovery couched in the rhetoric of science is to let it be known that the presumed fact can safely be used in debate, in practical projects, and so on. Knowledge claims are tacitly prefixed with a performative of trust" (Harré 1990: 97). This recalls debates concerning the subjective dimension of archaeological knowledge (Thompson 1956, Fritz and Plog 1970). Even more critical for my purposes, his analysis draws attention to the assumption of an evaluative community sharing an orientation toward a super-addressee that underpins conventional scientific writing. As James Deetz (1998b: 94) recognized, the dominant form of archaeological writing "seems to have been perpetuated by example; if that report is written in this fashion, then mine must be as well."

The site reports of the late twentieth century, despite having excised the forms of narration so visible in earlier epistolary reports, are narrative nonetheless. The narratives they relate are constructed dialogically within an evaluative community, and are unified by recourse to shared super-addressees. To make sense of Harré's argument, and this extension to archaeology, I need to return to the definition of narrative briefly considered in chapter 1. Archaeological discussions of narrative have made good use of the examples of analysis of historical narrative provided by Hayden White (1973, 1987). But White's identification of narrative with story severely limits the scope of discursive products that are under examination.

Gérard Genette (1980: 25–9, 1988: 13–20), from whose discussion of narrative I depart, emphasizes narrative statements, the way things are told, rather than narrative as either a sequence of events (story) or the act of telling, the two faces of historical narrative that interest White. Genette's focus is on the *relationships* between narrative, narrating, and story. While narrative and story can be related to each other in terms of tense and mood, in order to relate narrating (telling) to story and narrative, Genette needs to employ a concept of voice (1980: 212–62). While Genette's structuralist approach is fundamentally aligned with systems of literary analysis that Bakhtin critiques (Morson and Emerson 1990: 19), his discussion of voice usefully foregrounds an aspect of narrative that is left out of analyses that take narrative as story or text. Genette's discussion of voice calls attention to the subjective position of the narrating person. What he calls the "narrating situation" is the position that concerns contemporary archaeologists who are actively experimenting with different forms of writing.

Genette (1980: 215–27) demonstrates that, while the notion of narrating as telling a story predisposes us to assume that narrating follows story, in fact the "time of the narrating" expressed by the narrating voice can easily be predictive or take the form of a "live" running commentary. Archaeological narratives constructed to tell a story that is clearly marked as in the past (like the one that opens this chapter) are thus the product of a choice conditioned by the narrating situation. I could easily retell the story of Mantecales as a predictive narrative, and of course I did actually narrate Mantecales in the future during the excavations that took place in the summer of 1995. This kind of predictive narration is crucial to the social construction of meaning in the archaeological research process. It is part of the way we shape our understanding, it guides choices about what procedures to undertake as the work is ongoing, and it would be quite impossible to do archaeology without engaging in this kind of narrating.

Narration as running commentary is, I would argue, equally built in to our field practice. To adopt one particular time of narrating, the retrospective view back over a completed story would impede our ability to communicate the process through which we come to understand things. One of the losses in the shift from epistolary reports to the archaeological reports of the twentieth century has been the more complex representation of the time of narration that is provided by the use of letters and diaries (compare Genette 1980: 217–18). Experiments in providing access to narratives of ongoing time of research embodied in field diaries, videotapes, and other contemporaneous records promise to restore this lost narrative complexity (e.g. Stevanovic 2000, Wolle and Tringham 2000).

Archaeologists Writing Culture

The participants in the conference which resulted in *Writing Culture* (Clifford and Marcus 1986) were concerned to consider contextual, rhetorical, institutional, generic, political, and historical dimensions of ethnographic writing (Clifford 1986: 6). A critical claim made for this project was that such an inquiry was not simply an inquiry into formal poetics, but simultaneously a political critique. James Clifford (1983) had argued previously that ethnographic genres could be distinguished, at least partly, in terms of their rhetorical strategies. The four categories of ethnography he defined – experiential, interpretive, dialogic, and polyphonic – were a mapping of different kinds of claims of authority. As Paul Rabinow (1986: 245) notes, in Clifford's argument "it is hard not to read the history of anthropological writing as a loose progression toward dialogical and polyphonic textuality," with dialogic and polyphonic ethnographies presented in a more

positive light than temporally earlier, traditional experiential or interpretive ("realist") ethnographies.

Archaeology, of course, is distinct in practice from ethnography,
not foremost because of the lack of access to past speakers (which I
would argue is an illusory distinction), but rather because of its
inherent authorial multivocality, stemming from our collaboration in
research teams. While we can speak of contemporary archaeological
writing in terms of its alternative use of rhetoric of experience, interpretation, dialogue, and polyphony in examining archaeological textuality, it is probably more useful to take the question asked *of*
ethnography – what forms of authority are present in texts – rather
than the kinds of textual authority proposed *for* ethnography as a
guide to exploration. The principle evident differences among different forms of archaeological narratives are in the presence, number, and
status of speaking voices (compare Bapty 1989). If the traditional
research article can be seen as speaking in the first person plural, in
the process implicating readers as coauthors, it can be distinguished
from contemporary experimental writing that foregrounds a first-
person singular speaker in dialogue with other independent speakers
(as in the dialogue that opened this chapter), in the process preserv-
ing more of a sense of the collaborative nature of archaeological
knowledge construction. Archaeological dialogues raise the interesting question of responsibility of the writer – the "I" in first-person
narratives – to those represented, like characters in the novel.

More than in contemporary ethnographic writing (Tedlock 1995),
attempts at dialogue have been pervasive in archaeological experimentation with text (e.g. Bapty 1990, Bender 1998, Flannery 1976,
Hodder 1992, 1999, R. Joyce 1994). Authors of archaeological dialogues use two different strategies in creating the voices they put into
play. In some dialogues the characters are fictional constructs who
stand in for stereotypes, like Kent Flannery's Real Mesoamerican
Archaeologist, Skeptical Graduate Student, and Great Synthesizer. A
more recent example of this strategy is Matthew Johnson's character
Roger Beefy, "an undergraduate student at Northern University,
England" (1999: 3). The characters given voice in dialogues of this
kind tend to be contemporary with the archaeologist narrator, the
author of the text. The characters are generic stand-ins for the actual
interlocutors with whom the archaeologist talks things out in the
field, the lab, and the classroom.

Of course, the degree of freedom granted to these characters is
highly variable, and never goes so far as a total rejection of the author's
intent. Flannery's characters are generally acknowledged to be vividly

drawn portraits of veritably real people (so real that among specialists in Mesoamerica, it is common to hear them identified with specific named archaeologists). Other dialogic characters may not achieve
as great a degree of realism: Roger Beefy, despite being given a significant amount of biographical attention, remains a caricature, somewhat of an oaf, hooked on the physical practice of archaeology with
no understanding of the nuances of theory:

> Ah Roger, the eternal empiricist . . . Roger fell in love with archaeol-
> ogy when he was a child, scrambling up and down the ruins of local
> castles, burial mounds, and other sites. Roger spent a year after school
> before coming to Northern University digging and working in
> museums. Roger loves handling archaeological material, and is happi-
> est when drawing a section or talking about seriation techniques over
> a beer. Now, in his second year at Northern University, Roger has
> found himself in the middle of a compulsory "theory course". Full of
> twaddle about middle-range theory, hermeneutics and poststructural-
> ism, it seems to have nothing to do with the subject he loves. (Johnson
> 1999: 3)

Interestingly, just as Flannery (1976: 369) in the end identifies his
characters as all aspects of every archaeologist (perhaps to be taken as
typifying the narrator's own internal complexity), Johnson (1999: 186)
also identifies explicitly, if obliquely, with Roger Beefy in the end: "I
came to archaeology not quite as Roger Beefy, but as the 'dirt archaeologist' character who has been questioning things in this volume."
Projecting the archaeologist-author's own dilemmas onto crafted
characters serves both to externalize internal dialogues, and to a
certain extent insulates the narrator from dilemmas of auto-critique:
the impulse to clarify and defend (Wolf 1992: 116), and the suspicion
of strategic omissions.

Given the risks of attempting dialogue with unmasked projections
of internal voices, it is remarkable how common this strategy actually
is in archaeological writing. Ian Bapty (1990) presents the most openly
self-critical dialogue that is perhaps possible, not just for an archaeologist, but for any reflexive scholar. He populates his work, glossed
as a play, and presented as a transcription of a performance, with two
"voices," Inward and Outward, and a third person, "The Past," who
"is frequently referred to and seems always on the point of an entrance
she never makes" (Bapty 1990: 234). The topic of the dialogue
between Inward and Outward Voices is the emotions experienced
through engagement in archaeology and their suppression, or alter-
natively, their exploitation, in the service of rationality. As Inward

Voice virtually shrieks: "I am here all the time – though you try to ignore me. You cannot do anything without my involvement, and my advice, deny it as you will. I am part of your experience, and I am part of the past which you generate from that experience," railing against the untroubled speech of Outward Voice: "And yet, to merely acknowledge a certain emotional responsibility to the past is in a large degree to sidestep the issue of how emotion, in any constructive and practical sense, is actually to be incorporated into the process of archaeological interpretation" (Bapty 1990: 239).

Dialogues that give voice to the internal uncertainties of the archaeologist might be seen as an attempt to write into control the fluid knowledge construction that takes place as we work together (compare Hodder 1992: 158). My ability to provide a story line in the dialogue that opens this chapter retrospectively makes sense of an experience which was far more messy, and one in which I did not have the luxury of simply an internal debate. The dialogue I reframe took place as part of ongoing being-as-event that "cannot be transcribed in theoretical terms if it is not to lose the very sense of its being an event, that is, precisely that which the performed act knows answerably and with reference to which it orients itself" (Bakhtin 1993: 30–1). In archaeological practice, despite claims of hierarchical authority built into the language of the field (chapter 2), we produce our data in dialogue with others – collaborating colleagues, students, and specialists – of whom we are not the authors (although, as we will see in chapter 4, we are dialogically producing our selves as archaeologists in conversation with the same others).

The experience and its representation in language are each unique, but they are not incommensurate; they are related by the active process of giving value to the experience, of responding to it, and shaping it as meaningful. Bakhtin (1993: 31) argues that the re-description of "Being-as-event," experience, "attempts to describe not the world produced by that act, but the world in which that act becomes answerably aware of itself," and takes on value. One of the things dialogues accomplish in archaeology is to represent the social nature of the creation of archaeological knowledge. Beyond a simple description of what happened, dialogic narratives restore a sense of the negotiation of one understanding out of the many possible in any real archaeological situation.

Many of the archaeological dialogues that present fictional characters may be seen, and at times even acknowledged, as projections of multiple perspectives that the archaeologist narrator can adopt herself. Other dialogues represent what are clearly meant to be voices of contrast. In a "Dialogue about the relationship between data and theory" (Hodder 1999: 64–5) the characters Tester, Fitter, and Dialectical thinker exist as materializations of the perspectives of distinct views within archaeology. Fitter is marked as closest to the position of the archaeologist author by references back to material presented in the preceding chapter. The standpoint of Fitter is as respondent to the initiating objection raised by Tester, who resists the differentiation being made between the hermeneutic and hypothesis-testing approaches. The debate between two voices, one that of the narrator, the other of an imagined critic, is relayed to a third voice, Dialectical thinker, who takes the dialogic position vacated by Tester. Surprisingly, it is this third voice who has the last word, and not simply as an affirmation (compare Hodder 1992), but in contradiction to the voice closest to that of the author. "Between these two judgments there exists a specific logical relationship: one is the negation of the other.... Both these judgments must be embodied, if a dialogic relationship is to arise between them and toward them ... if these two judgments are separated into two different utterances by two different subjects, then dialogic relationships do arise" (Bakhtin 1984: 183). By putting the last words in the mouth of another character who is allowed to sustain a conflicting point of view, this dialogue moves toward the requirements for real polyphony.

Contradiction to the voice of the narrator is more consistently represented by the use, not of fictive voices, but of quotation from actual persons, positioned for strategic effect by the composer of a work. This strategy is not so far from the use of citation in traditional archaeological writing, but it attempts to give greater scope to the alternative speaking voice by changing the temporal relationships between the author and those cited. The new chronotope created is one in which, rather than having a succession of statements over extended time, we are presented with a simultaneity between voices of those in the disciplinary past and those in a present tense.

The creation of surreal effects in dialogues that split the writer in two, or that relay imagined critique and response, while risking flattening representation through unsympathetic stereotyping, has the advantage of clearly signaling its constructed, artificial nature. Dialogues using the voices of real persons risk representing the opinions of the author as those of someone else, deferring responsibility for the position advocated. In my constructed dialogue on the life of Dorothy Popenoe, an early-twentieth-century archaeologist working in Honduras, I quoted a multitude of voices representing Popenoe (R. Joyce 1994). By embedding these voices in explicit reflection on the challenge of reconstructing a view of a woman's life from fragmentary materials, I attempted to make clear that I was not claiming authority by citing the words of others. This goal was advanced by the contradictions within the sources I could cite.

Because this work started as a computerized hypertext, in its original versions it actively resisted priorities of multiple kinds, presenting readers with an initial choice of multiple entry points into the text that were so densely interlinked that no one *sequence* of voices was likely to consistently emerge. In the printed medium, I was able to simulate this effect by starting the story three different times. The decision to subvert the standard use of biography in writing archaeological history (Givens 1992) dictated my decision to maintain the immediacy of different points of view. It also required that I clearly define my own standpoint, in the process of which I linked myself and my subject in a single temporal frame: "my own engagement with Popenoe began when, as a novice in Honduras, I first was told a slightly inaccurate version of her death . . . she preceded me at my dissertation site . . . it was only in researching the Peabody's Honduran collections that I began to realize how much of her legacy had been lost" (R. Joyce 1994: 53–4).

Similar care in positioning the writer and others placed in dialogue marks perhaps the longest sustained use of dialogues in archaeology to date, Barbara Bender's (1998) *Stonehenge: Making Space*. Bender published real/constructed dialogues – real in that they are between named positioned persons, but constructed through editing and in some cases – where the dialogue was multi-exchange email – through a process not unlike the composition of thoroughly fictional dialogues discussed above. Bender (1998: 11) writes:

> I wanted to use the dialogues to question and to open up discussions of matters raised in the different chapters. I found the dialogues exhilarating precisely because they were dialogues, the arguments could move backwards and forwards, they could be critical and constructive, could offer alternative ways of thinking about things, bring in other case-studies, and they could also – *although the people involved could not appreciate this* – play off each other. . . . It is my book, I take responsibility, I set the agenda, but while I structure the dialogues and ask the questions, I cannot control the answers. So, although there are closures, things go off in unpredicted directions and expose the possibilities of other agendas, other books. (emphasis added)

This places quite precisely the central issues involved in creating dialogues from the material provided by other speakers. The juxtapositions created are constructive of new utterances. As Bakhtin reminds us in his discussion of the total context of communication, each utterance in its specific context is unique. The people quoted in the dialogues have no control over the new context of communication in which the words they are credited with appear. The opinions that we might take from these dialogues should be assigned to the author, as she rightly notes in accepting responsibility for the final work.

> We must pause briefly on the author, who is the creator of the work, and the distinctive form of [her] activity. We find the author *outside* the work as a human being living [her] own biographical life. But we also meet [her] as the creator of the work itself, although [she] is located outside the chronotopes represented in [her] work, [she] is as it were tangential to them. We meet [her] (that is we sense [her] activity) most of all in the composition of the work: it is [she] who segments the work into parts. . . . The author moves freely in [her] own time: [she] can begin [her] story at the end, in the middle, or at any moment of the events represented . . . [she] does [her] observing from [her] own unresolved and still evolving contemporaneity. (Bakhtin 1981: 254–5)

Having other voices in the text does create greater heteroglossia, as these speakers say things in their own unique dialects. But it is questionable whether it truly introduces polyphony. "In a monologic work, only the author . . . retains the power to express a truth directly. The truth of the work is his or her truth and all other truths are merely 'represented' . . . by contrast, in a polyphonic work the form-shaping ideology itself *demands* that the author cease to exercise monologic control" (Morson and Emerson 1990: 238). While Bender does not control the answers to the questions (in the sense that her respondents can say what they want) she does control them through editing and through contextualization.

> Even in the segmentation of a modern literary work we sense the chronotope of the represented world as well as the chronotope of the readers and creators of the work . . . every work has a *beginning* and an *end*, the event represented likewise has a beginning and an end, but these beginnings and ends lie in different worlds, in different chronotopes that can never fuse with each other or be identical to each other. (Bakhtin 1981: 254–5)

The power of segmentation is an explicit topic touched on in one of the dialogues, with Nick Merriman of the Museum of London,

host for an experimental, multivocalic exhibit on Stonehenge whose
genesis is richly documented in the book (Bender 1998: 145–71). In
response to Bender's query, "Do you think that there are tensions
... between throwing it open for different voices to be heard, acting
as mediator or enabler, and creating the overall structure?", Merriman
replies (in part):

> That's a difficult one, and I've agonised over it quite a lot ... you're
> acting much more like an editor, or a conductor of an orchestra. . . .
> You have to be explicit to the people you're working with about your
> agenda ... if you're working from a critical perspective, and you're
> aware of the position you're adopting, and you're willing, as part of
> that, to embrace as many points of view as possible, and to discuss it
> with people, then it's OK. . . . I don't think it matters that you're quite
> heavily involved in creating the overall shape. *Ultimately, in a way, it's
> your job to do this, and you have to be prepared not to hide behind
> people.* (Bender 1998: 214–15; emphasis added)

You have to be prepared not to hide behind people. Bender (1998:
215) annotates this point with a quotation: "We are obliged to share
authority with both subject and reader, but equally cannot evade
the authority of authorship." She further shifts the context of the
comment by inserting a reference to another point in her text at the
end of her question. There (Bender 1998: 253) she asks of her role as
exhibit coordinator,

> Is this not just another form of power? One moment I am totally
> involved in putting together the exhibition, I am engaged and partisan.
> At another, the exhibition becomes this chapter, I don my ethnogra-
> pher's hat, stand back from the action and try to account for what is
> happening. What is concrete becomes abstract; what might seem objec-
> tive to the groups involved, becomes subjective and relative. . . . All one
> can do is recognise and reluctantly accept that one's thoughts and
> actions are ambiguous and often contradictory, but that one should try,
> as much as possible, not to speak for, but to speak with and to people
> – try to invest in dialogues, rather than subsume others within
> monologues.

If the diffusion of authority promised by transcribing dialogues is
not really achieved, even in the densest and most generous use that
can be made of the speaker's own words, what consequences follow?
The language in informal dialogues does seem less open to accountability. What is said may be looser, reference may be dispensed with
or very general. Bender blends the pure looseness of her dialogues

with conventions of academic citation, inserting footnotes that gesture outward toward published works, lending the conversations an appearance of greater reliability. While this has the advantage of establishing another layer of intertextuality, the result can sometimes be a hybrid whose immediacy of voice is compromised by greater service to the conductor's intent.

One example may make clearer what I mean here. In the transcription of a conversation with Ruth Tringham, I was startled to see my own name emerge in a critical comment:

> BB: . . . Rosemary Joyce talks about complementarity in the portrayal of men and women in Mayan iconography, and yes, the women are portrayed, but most times they're kneeling to the man and making an offering! The women and their work are totally essential, but there's a power imbalance.
> RT: In a more recent paper, Rosemary does bring in hierarchy (Bender 1998: 88; the insertion of [Joyce] in the final utterance has been omitted).

My first reaction in reading this exchange was much like what one feels when overhearing a negative comment in person. My second was that the characterization of my work was entirely wrong, since there has never been a time when I wasn't talking about hierarchy. My third reaction was that the description of Maya representation was thoroughly inaccurate; even if we leave aside all the three-dimensional figurines (in which women are shown as independent subjects, and therefore cannot ever be "kneeling to the man and making an offering"), the fact is that even in monumental art images showing a kneeling woman holding materials next to a standing man (not kneeling "to" him, nor necessarily always "offering" him things, since these are both interpretations of a static image) are a numerical minority. My fourth reaction was amusement at my own instant retreat into objectivism. And then I stopped reacting and asked myself what my evaluative response to this snippet of dialogue could tell me about the nature of transcribed dialogues as a whole.

Why did an offhand comment in a conversation bother me? Well, obviously, despite the representation of this as a conversation, I was reading it as something more formal. Not only was this conversation embedded in a book, and thus from my reaction made less ephemeral and more authoritative; it was provided with numbered footnotes which I did not reproduce above. The first of these, following the initial paraphrase of Bender's reading of my work, cited two articles

(R. Joyce 1992a, 1993b). The second, inserted at the end of the first sentence of Tringham's response, cited a third (R. Joyce 1996a). Presumably, Bender did know what articles she had in mind in her critique (although the fact remains that those articles do not deny gender hierarchy, and in fact argue for the *erasure* of images of active and independent women in artworks created by and for the reigning nobility). But the addition of a reference to Ruth Tringham's informal comment is the act of the omniscient author. While this looks like an exchange about my work, it is in fact a short monologue in which the character RT is allowed to play the advocate for a narrative of my progressive enlightenment.

And this is where my overreaction (and I am sure, dear reader, you were thinking that by now) tells me something very interesting. I was taking this at surface value as a dialogue, despite the work Bender invested in telling me otherwise, *including the destabilizing insertion of footnotes in what purports to be a transcription of an informal conversation*, and despite my own considerable investment in theoretical perspectives which would suggest that even the original conversation was a formal representation. My feelings were hurt that friends of mine would publish a negative comment without letting me explain. (Since, ironically, the writing of the article published in 1996 preceded the others, having been presented at a conference in 1990, and having languished in the hard roads of antifeminist reviewing until a new publication opportunity presented itself, I could only despair at the apparent notion that I didn't get wise until the later date.) But there are in fact no friends of mine in this text; there are simply characters furnished with extraordinarily vivid languages through the appropriation of the words of others. I think Bender would agree that ultimately, the dialogues are as much her writing as the less dialogic parts of the work.

My error in reception of such archaeological experiment is not unique; Mary Beaudry (personal communication 2001) reports that some readers have asked about the whereabouts of the journals she imagined in her exquisite dialogue in the form of journal entries that might have been written by residents on a New England farm explored archaeologically. Beaudry (1998: 20) deliberately chose to present the multiple first-person stories she wrote in the form of journals: "why not use the existence of Offin Boardman's journal as a taking-off point for 'discovering' personal accounts kept by other people who spent part of their lives at the site?" The form she adopts is a four-part dialogue: Nathaniel Tracy's words from 1779–88 link to Mary Lee Tracy's entries from 1775 (her marriage to him) through

1796 (his death) and 1797, when she sells the farm to Offin Board-man; his entries from 1797 through 1810, including references to his wife Sally; and Sally's from 1799 to 1811, after Offin's death. The voices are each distinct.

Beaudry (1998: 20), noting especially the absence of women's accounts, decided to provide them: "I've often thought how mar-velous it would be if other people . . . had left us journals recordings their observations and the details of their day-to-day lives." Interest-ingly, one of the narratives she presents *is* that of Offin Boardman, where she includes "real" and "imagined" entries, using typography to distinguish them. The "real" entries are derived in the first place from a copy of a partial transcript, emphasizing the coherence introduced by the retrospective shaping of fragments of experience common to all archaeological writing, foregrounded in experimental forms like this.

Beaudry (1998: 27) based the "voice" of Nathaniel on a letter, and the two women on contemporary women diarists: "I used my general impressions . . . rather than any specific diary, noting especially the recurring tropes employed by the diarists, in creating voices" for the women. While this allowed for the realization of profound het-eroglossia, again, the question of actual polyphony is somewhat less clear. The subject matter of the journal entries was entirely determined by the interests of contemporary archaeology. Beaudry (1998: 30) grounded her imagined journal entries in the features that were iden-tified through excavation: "My aim has been to link the diary entries as closely as possible to the archaeological record . . . as a way of explaining the presence of particular features or artifacts." This self-imposed constraint can be seen as an expression of the author's responsibility *as an archaeologist* to speak not only for the past human subjects, but also for the nonhuman subjects that mediate between them and us. The constraint that comes with the archaeological terri-tory is a recurrent issue in contemporary experimental writing, both as the enabling ground for imagination, and as a limiting factor around which we are obliged to tack (Wylie 1989, 1992a).

Adrian and Mary Praetzellis (1998) provide a wonderful example of a dialogue based precisely on the notion that there would be a gap in perspective concerning material remains between past users of these things and present-day archaeologists. Set up as a dialogue between the archaeologist and a Gold Rush merchant and lawyer, Josiah Gallup, it is framed as an intervention in the presentation of a traditional research paper at the annual meeting of the Society for Historical Archaeology.

Archaeologist: "What do these artifacts mean? What are they telling us?"

Gallup: "Now, what nonsense is this? How may a plate be said to *tell* us anything? In all my travels I've never heard of communion between items of dinner ware and diners. Or discussions between bowls. Of heated debates between a tureen and a slop jar, perhaps." (Praetzellis and Praetzellis 1998: 88–9)

The Gallup character goes on to challenge the meaning of the dinnerware, noting that he bought the European-style wares and therefore they could not imply assimilation by the Chinese boarders who lived at the site. Both voices end their presentations of what in fact are alternative explanations – one more informed by historical information embodied in the character – at the same time. The merchant speaks the actual opinions of the authors, who thus place the archaeologist character in the position of a parody – of themselves, or a less informed self. But the merchant also speaks for the integrity of the material remains, as a form of utterance continuously moving forward through time, available for new dialogic engagement.

Like Bapty's dialogue between the archaeologist's two voices, this dialogue is presented as a performance in the space–time of the archaeological meeting. Implicitly, this circumstance recognizes the position from which authority is constructed, while introducing a trace of the verbal exchanges through which archaeological knowledge is constructed, something that normally is excluded from representation. Dialogic works that cite words of known persons often engage with the question of the authority of a speaker over the interpretation of his or her words. Julia Costello (1998: 66; see also 2000: 163) cites Anna Deveare Smith as support for the position that "the words that informants use in telling their stories are perfect for conveying their message: they are not improved by being paraphrased, condensed, summarized, or cleaned up."

Costello is concerned with the multiplicity of stories that could be evoked by material remains of past lives. In her work on Italian bread ovens in California, she found that in transcribing interviews she

began to appreciate other stories about the ovens, in addition to my questions about technologies, processes, and ethnic affiliations. And, I began to learn that the stories that informants want to tell about the ovens may constitute, ultimately, more valuable records of these historical features than the information I had been asking about. They reflect those aspects of bread baking that were important to the people who used the ovens, exactly those aspects that anthropologists try to discover and understand. (1998: 66)

Costello recognizes that utterances are acts of communication seeking an evaluative response. She raises the issue of whether the speaker can finalize the meaning of the utterance in a way that should be more highly valued than might be provided by continued dialogic engagement. She includes in her text her own utterances in dialogue with those of the narratives she reports (Costello 1998: 71–3). Her voice as archaeologist is objective; it summarizes and generalizes. It introduces other motivations beyond those acknowledged in the individual oral narratives she reproduces. Her voice provides a description of the scientific principles involved in the functioning of bread ovens that is an utterance in a dialogue distinct from the experiential one of the bakers. The archaeologist's voice engages dialogically with other external utterances: studies of bread-baking ovens in Quebec and on railroad sites, as well as two histories of Italian immigration, one specific to San Francisco. Costello demonstrates why, although the words that speakers use may be the best ones to represent their speaking position, as producers of texts, archaeologists continue to introduce other voices beyond those of the original speakers. As Adrian Praetzellis (1998: 1) argues, what we construct

> is *the site's* story in the sense that the story emerges from the site. But this is not to say that some specific story lurks within the soil and the artifacts waiting to be freed by the archaeologist. On the contrary. The site contains many potential stories, but every one is a product of the archaeological imagination that pulls together historical and archaeological facts into an interpretation that is more than the sum of the parts of which it is made and more than its excavator can document in the usual way.

How close, in fact, can we come to letting loose autonomous voices in an archaeological text? The experiment of providing on-line access to the findings of the Çatalhöyük project, including explicit engagement with other electronic communities interested in the site, points to a medium and a practice that is beginning to address this possibility (Hodder 1999: 124–7, 180–4, 192, Wolle and Tringham 2000). The next two chapters consider specific examples of electronic hypertexts that, not coincidentally, introduce autonomous voices into archaeological interpretations.

4

A Second Voice: *Crafting Cosmos*

Writing in the classical and Western traditions is supposed to have a voice and therefore to speak to its reader. A *printed book* generally speaks with a single voice and assumes a consistent character, a persona, before its audience. . . . In the Middle Ages, unrelated texts were often bound together, and texts were often added in the available space in a volume years or decades later. Even in the early centuries of printing, it was not unusual to put unrelated works between two covers. However, it is natural to think of any book, written or printed, as a verbal unit. For the book *is* a physical unit; its pages are sewn or glued together and then bound into a portable whole. Should not all the words inside proceed from one unifying idea and stand in the same rhetorical relationship to the reader? From *Writing Space* by Jay David Bolter, cited in Joyce, Guyer, and Joyce 2000[7]

Third Dialogue: Crafting Crafting Cosmos: *A Hypermedia Exploration of Materiality and the Dialogic Creation and Re-Creation of Classic Maya Society*

Jeanne Lopiparo

Preamble: Now with Three Layers of Metalanguage!

The title of this section rings with the double-speak of a metalanguage that announces that we are about to analyze analysis, think about thinking, or write about writing. This should be the part where I cleverly avoid the expected rhetorical trap, but instead I'll be serving up not just one, not just two – but *three* layers of metalanguage! For interwoven in this project are multiple threads of argumentation that share a fundamental concern with the production of culture through the everyday, discursive, and nondiscursive inscriptional practices of agents – both past and present – in their creation of and interaction with material culture. The threefold purpose of this discussion is: (1) in general, to talk about how forms of writing are inseparable from the purported "content" or meaning of that writing (White 1987)– that the knowledge constructed through inscriptional practices is inseparable from the practices themselves, and these practices are in turn situated in and structured by the relations of power and habitus of the scribe; (2) specifically, to instantiate these assertions through the explication of a hypermedia project, *Crafting Cosmos: The Production of Social Memory in Everyday Life Among the Classic Maya*, which explores the production of our own culture and the construction of modern understandings of society through the production of archaeological knowledge about or "writing" of Maya prehistories; (3) while simultaneously attempting to embody through hypermedia the parallel argument that the Maya discursively crafted their own culture (in part) through analogous inscriptional practices and ways of "crafting" the material culture that we recover and interpret as archaeologists. Thus from the bottom up, we have the archaeology, an archaeology of the archaeology, and an archaeology of the archaeology of archaeology.

All three of these strands are interwoven about a common concern with the constitution of culture through the everyday, commonplace practices (both discursive and nondiscursive) of agents – particularly those inscriptional practices which, broadly construed, would include any act of "storage" through which ideas are manifested or crafted in material culture – into artifacts which then both serve as mnemonics for and embodiments of those ideas and enter into potentially infinite dialogues and webs of signification. Within archaeology these concerns have been addressed in recent approaches to household archaeology that focus on reconstructing "thick descriptions" of everyday practices and microscale processes – portraying their richness and variability (e.g. Tringham 1991, 1994, 1995), while at the same time addressing how these practices have continuity through time and result in the persistence of shared culture (both material and otherwise) and structures of social organization (Gillespie 2000a, Joyce and Gillespie 2000).

These central themes are reflected in the original title of the hypermedia project: *Crafting Cosmos: The Production of Social Memory in Everyday Life Among the Classic Maya*. The title emphasizes that

culture and society are continually "made," that they are in a continual state of flux, an unending process of becoming – while the pre-
ponderance of active verbs reveals an implicit focus on human agency
based in the post-structuralist traditions of practice (Bourdieu 1977)
and structuration theories (Giddens 1979, 1984). As I will argue
below, within the theoretical frameworks that posit the "constitution
of society" through a dialectical relationship between structure and
agency, the relative emphasis placed on agency, free will, or innovation, versus structure, constraint, or stasis, is one of the major axes of
differentiation amongst post-structuralist theoreticians (an axis which
I refer to as the PRACTICE THEORY LIGHT ↔ PRACTICE THEORY DARK
continuum). While "Crafting..." and "Constitution of..." both
connote "making," the more active and embodied tenor of the former
occupies a position on the agency end of this continuum when compared with the politico-jural shadings of the latter. Similarly, "...
Cosmos" and "... Society" both connote the structures of thought –
the universe of what is thinkable and, perhaps more importantly, what
is unthinkable – but the degree of formalization and fixedness of these
structures implied by each word is again vastly different.

Much of this differentiation stems from embedded assumptions
about the effectiveness of the modes of inscription – particularly
writing versus orality, imagery, and materiality – in fixing or maintaining the intended meanings and power structures of the "authors"
of those inscriptions. This cognitive schism is inscribed in our cosmos
as the almost universally reified differentiation of historic and prehistoric. Thus everyday practices that involve the production, decoration, or use of a pot are not deemed to be as instrumental in the
production and reproduction of the structures of society, than if an
authority were to write about the rules and meanings of their production and use. But even assuming that a potter does adhere to a set
of rules in the creation of that pot – rules based in a habitus of aesthetics, function, utility, and in the demands and expectations of
others – these rules themselves would be dialogically constituted
through their enactment, and often, their transformation. Writing
them would not necessarily preserve, determine, or constrain their
further enactment or instantiation any more than other forms of discourse (e.g. orality) or nondiscursive interaction with and evaluation
of the maker, the pot, or its various users.

Part 1: Materiality and the Dialogic Creation and Re-Creation of Society

If we consider the creation of material culture to be analogous to Barthes's "texts" or Bakhtin's "utterances," we must also consider the implications of Barthes's "Death of the Author" (1977a) (which in the case of archaeological artifacts is both figuratively and literally true) and Bakhtin's conception of the inherent interindividuality and unfinalizability (after Morson and Emerson 1990: 37, 129) of the utterance. Artifacts – as past utterances – were not monologically authored by their crafter, but rather were shaped and dialogically constituted by the assumption of the active understanding and participation of the addressee (for example, those who would interact with them). Bakhtin's notion that utterances also assume a "super-addressee," an ideal listener who would respond with perfect understanding, allows for the intent of the creator. Archaeologists, in a sense, frequently position themselves as reconstructing the true meaning as a sort of anachronistic "super-addressee" by uncovering the "true" or "intended" meaning of the creator of archaeological objects. As Bakhtin makes clear, however, neither the author nor the addressee "own" the meaning, but rather it is created dialogically in multiple contexts (Morson and Emerson 1990: 127–30). As Barthes says: "the text's unity lies not in its origin, but in its destination" (1977a: 148).

While these material traces become vehicles for social memory (Connerton 1989, Hendon 2000, R. Joyce 2000b), their meaning is never fixed, but in a perpetual state of becoming – in an eternal dialogue with what came before (both the intended and unintended meanings of its producer and the circumstances of its production), the particular present of those who are interacting with it (addressees in the Bakhtinian sense, or readers/writers in the Barthesian sense), and its perceived future – its potential purpose or uses vis-à-vis future circumstances and audiences. Its significance is therefore constantly negotiated, its meanings conserved or manipulated, maintained, or contested.

"The social life of things" (Appadurai 1986)

The idea that material culture, from artifacts to architecture, has dynamic histories (Tringham 1991, Weiner 1992) introduces the structured and structuring role of material culture in everyday life. The significance of material culture in the embodiment, storage, transmission, and negotiation of social structures, values, and identities has been emphasized by practice theorists, ethnographers and archaeologists alike (Appadurai 1986, Bourdieu 1973, 1977, Donley-Reid 1990, Giddens 1981, 1984, R. Joyce 1992b, 1996a, 1998a, Love 1999, Miller 1998, Moore 1986, Pearson and Richards 1994, Pred 1984, 1990, Rodman 1992, Weiner 1992). The "life-histories" of material remains – from their production, through the multiple activities in which they were involved, to their eventual discard – have become the object of detailed analysis by archaeologists, many of whom situate themselves within post-structuralist or post-processual discourses (Hodder 1987, Tringham 1994, Stevanovic 1997, Hendon 2000). But even archaeologists who in no way profess an interest in narrativizing the past approach material culture not only as an entrée to social processes, but in essence as a life-history of material culture that is made to "stand in for" – or tell the story of – a faceless aggregate people who created and used those objects. These life-histories focus on such milestones as an artifact's birth (production), marriage (exchange), work (use-life), death (disposal/deposition) – even its afterlife (post-depositional processes) – and *especially* its reincarnation (archaeological resurrection through excavation, recovery, interpretation, and reconstruction). Thus, for example, the fate of an artifact through the exchange of material culture – even when reconstructed in the most scientific language of parts per billion of antimony – stands in for the social relations between producer and consumer, with assumptions about the value or status ascribed to that object often determining the interpretation of the relations of power between the two groups.

Given the many "roles" that artifacts play, it is interesting that an inordinate emphasis is placed on the processes of an object's birth/production – as if the moment of creation determines the meaning and value of an object. From an ecologically or economically instrumentalist perspective, production answers the question of value through the lens of necessity. From an ideational viewpoint, an object's creation holds the potential of revealing the "intent" of the creator, and thus the ideas, structures of thoughts, and relations of power that were manifested in these particular objects. Perhaps most important is the association of production or creation itself with economic or ideological power, either as control of the means of production or as the privileged capacity of creator and therefore author. But with the "The Death of the Author," we must consider that the importance placed on the processes of an artifact's creation belies the subjective (and intersubjective) nature of objects. As with texts, the creator does not determine meaning or value, but rather meanings are continually created and re-created through space and time and with relationships with different social actors.

In recognizing the importance of our complex constructions and reconstructions of self and society through the creation of and interaction with the material world, practice theories provide a framework for archaeologists to address social processes at multiple scales of organization through the artifacts with which they are most concerned. Practice theory and structuration-based multiscalar approaches allow for – and, in fact, require – the integration of daily practices and larger-scale changes in sociopolitical structures and environment by positing the mechanisms through which they do not simply interact, but are mutually constitutive. There can be no culture or social structures without their continual production and reproduction by agents, while these agents act within the discursive and nondiscursive constraints, shared expectations, and traditions of their particular histories and relations of power. Thus multiple levels or scales of social organization are not simply microcosms, with the "bottom tier" mimicking large-scale structures and relations of power. In their daily practices, the inhabitants of domestic sites both (re)produce and modify these larger-scale social structures, acting often in cooperation with multiple larger corporate groups according to shared interests, affiliations, histories, and expectations – but sometimes at odds with them. It is this practice-based conceptualization of the continual "work" of constituting culture that highlights the importance of the household and everyday practices, and shifts the focus from what these social groups are – as some kind of manifestation or microcosm of a preexisting, monolithic social order – to what households do to produce and reproduce culture in the processes of producing and reproducing themselves.

Households as knowledge object and object lesson:
the constitution of knowledge and archaeologists' responsibility
to the past

In order to break into the notion that households were not somehow all structurally and functionally the same, we must, following Rodman (1992), investigate them as both multilocal and multivocal – as loci for the construction and negotiation of multiple, complex, and often conflicting meanings, identities, and social relations. This complex notion of space as place, where multiple social identities are enacted through interaction with the material world (Rodman 1992, Tringham 1994, Pearson and Richards 1994, Hendon 1999, Gillespie 2000b, R. Joyce 2000b, Joyce and Hendon 2000), requires the fine-grained archaeological methodologies, analyses, and reconstructions of activities and uses of material culture that have been developed within the framework of household archaeology (e.g., Tringham 1991, 1994, Hodder 1997).

Rodman (1992: 649) argues that in order to hear all of the diverse and discordant voices, we must listen with all of our senses to the "narratives of places." Tringham has similarly argued that archaeologists must explore the stories of the many inhabitants of the household – that in order to engender prehistory, we must envisage "households with faces" (1991). Several other contributors to feminist archaeology have also advocated the use of narrative in the representation of archaeological data (R. Joyce 1998b, Spector 1993), with an understanding that in order to enrich our understanding of households in the past, we must acknowledge – in our methodologies, interpretations, and representations – the diversity of possible experiences of place.

Advocacy of the multivocalic creation of embodied prehistories parallels larger ethical debates within archaeology centering around issues of representation and the role, authority, and accountability of archaeologists in reconstructing the past (Wylie 1992b, 1995, Deloria 1992, Schmidt and Patterson 1995, R. Joyce 1999a). But foregrounding archaeologists' responsibility and answerability to multiple interested publics – and acknowledging that these interests are often conflicting – has launched vehement counter-critiques bemoaning the imperilment of academic freedom and scientific rigor in the face of the politicization of archaeology. Both Tringham (1991) and R. Joyce (1998b) have anticipated empiricist criticisms about the slippery slope of relativism and the validity or truth-value of such "storytelling" by arguing that given that our underlying assumptions and interests necessarily guide our research and interpretation, multiple perspectives can only enrich our understanding of the past – and are, in fact, necessary to capture the plurality of lived experience. Following Harding's (1991) advocacy of "strong objectivity," R. Joyce (1998b, see chapter 5) argues that we have an extraordinary "responsibility to the autonomous materiality" of the archaeological record, and must counter accounts that either ignore or are inconsistent with it. She points out that, in fact, feminist approaches are "particularly appropriate ... because the feminist project is one that specifically profits from the reworking of the suppressed aspects of materiality":

The residue of some people's actions are treated as normative, and the residue of other people's actions are divergence from those norms. Much of the "data" necessary to authorize different narratives about the past may already be available in the noise. . . . One implication of the commitment to material responsibility is that no archaeological narrative can ever be presented as closed. Recursive attention to variation previously set aside can always permit other materially responsible narratives, that through their accumulation result in denser, less deterministic, and hence more realistic stories about the past. The openness of narrative is something to be celebrated, not something to be feared.

Thus in order to account more responsibly for the situatedness of all knowledge construction and the diversity and conflict of lived experiences, we should not only seek plurality, openness, and dialogue in the many voices that might recursively contribute to all stages of archaeological research, but also seek this plurality in our representations of the past.

Part 2: Crafting *Crafting Cosmos*

There is neither a first nor a last word and there are no limits to the dialogic context (it extends into the boundless past and the boundless future). Even *past* meanings, that is, those born in the dialogue of past centuries, can never be stable (finalized, ended once and for all) – they will always change (be renewed) in the process of subsequent, future development of the dialogue. At any moment in the development of the dialogue there are immense, boundless masses of forgotten contextual meanings, but at certain moments of the dialogue's subsequent development along the way they are recalled and invigorated in renewed form (in a new context). **Nothing is absolutely dead**: every meaning will have its homecoming festival. **The problem of *great time*.** ("Methodology for the Human Sciences," Bakhtin 1986: 170)

"Nothing is absolutely dead . . ."

Though this could be the battle cry of archaeologists, we have nonetheless tended to downplay all these other aspects of the ongoing dialogue – the continual processes of creation through which material culture and its meanings are constituted – and particularly, the role of material culture in constructing our own conceptions of society. *Crafting Cosmos* is meant to encompass two seemingly disparate time-spaces, but I am arguing that they are not only analogous but intricately and inextricably intertwined. In other words, the constitution of society through dialogic interactions with material culture continues today. In the case of archaeology, the fact that this material is the *same* material culture that was instrumental in constituting past societies, epitomizes Bakhtin's assertion that "Nothing is absolutely dead."

"The problem of great time ..."

The use of analogy to try to make sense of past societies presents the perpetual problem of re*constructing* past societies in our image. Certainly there are rigorous criteria for validity and versimilitude, and all explanations are not created equal, but the problem with versimilitude is the degree to which our own habitus shapes our conceptions of the "limits of the possible." What seems commonsensical, parsimonious, or a matter of simple rationality or utility to us, must be viewed in light of the astute and now common critique of instrumentalist logic and rationalist or utilitarian explanation – that utility itself is socially constructed (e.g., Sahlins 1976: 12). So the problem becomes how to create multiple, unfinalized, and even conflicting narratives about past societies that reflect the conflicts of lived experiences through different perspectives and do not necessarily adhere to our limited, situated view of "the possible."

Hypermedia and multivocality

If we are to take seriously the ethical implications of Bakhtinian dialogism, we must critically consider the manner in which archaeologists monologize the past. Implicit in Bakhtin's ethics is a mandate to reconsider the methodological implications of how we write the past, in order to replace the practices that (re)present a closed and monologized view of past societies, with forms of representation that allow for both the inherent dialogism of multiple, often contradictory, lived experiences and our multiple and often contradictory means of understanding them. By considering the traces, mnemonics, embodiments, or "artifacts" of thought as situated in their particular contexts through a thick description of everyday life, and by expanding our notions of the limits of the possible to consider and account for multiple conceptions of past societies, we can approach a nonmonologized view of the past. But if there is (was) no singular meaning, we face the challenge of conveying this polyphony – not just through multiple interpretations but through multiple presentations and the creation of openings and unexpected questions.

> *"Let us first posit the image of a triumphal plural"*
> *(Barthes 1975:5)*

The discourses surrounding hypertext repeatedly return to its role in the ethics of knowledge creation – particularly in its potential to produce writerly texts that blur the boundaries between author and audience (Landow 1992, Tringham 1998; see chapter 5). By creating openings for multiple (often seemingly infinite) possible readings, the authority created by traditional linear argumentation – the narrative tropes typical of academic writings used to advance particular (often monologic) arguments – can be subverted and even exploded (note, for example the revolutionary rhetoric used here, – a good place in hypertext to point outward [or inward] to Hayden White's arguments, critiquing my own bluster). The methods of destabilizing master narratives inhere in the multiple and elaborately constructed means of navigating hypermedia projects.

ELABORATELY CONSTRUCTED...

This last phrase, of course, confronts us with the problem that the alleged freedoms of these post-structuralist arguments are, in fact, made by their structures. All of the possibilities – the links, the content, the means of navigating, and the pathways within the realm of a CD-ROM, for example, are "elaborately constructed" or orchestrated, often by single authors (though some argue that this boundedness is undermined in the case of the World Wide Web), which evokes the question raised in chapter 1: whether this type of multivocality is *really* polyphonic or merely "multiple instances of the same language." The argument that a commitment to multivocality replaces the rule of one with the rules of many is based on a belief that even a "single-authored" work can be (or even *necessarily* is) polyphonic. "Thus is revealed the total existence of writing: a text is made of multiple writings, drawn from many cultures and entering into mutual relations of dialogue, parody, contestation, but there is one place where this multiplicity is focused and that place is the reader, not, as was hitherto said, the author" (Barthes 1977a: 148). The work of monologizing a text – the degree to which "[t]he writer mystifies the production of meaning, making it something finished, preconceived and objectified, rather than a product of intellectual labour" (Olsen 1990: 176) – is itself a form of argumentation.

"To render the familiar strange . . ." (White 1978: 256): Or, common sense is neither common nor sensical. Discuss . . .

"human knowledge cannot participate in the World's becoming except through a series of successive metalanguages, each of which is alienated in the moment which determines it . . . the semiologist is a man who expresses his future death in the very terms in which he has named and understood the world" (Barthes 1990: 293–4, quoted in Olsen 1990: 174).

In her response in the *New York Times* to the honor of topping the list of "Bad Writers" in the conservative journal *Philosophy and Literature*, Judith Butler (1999) makes explicit the political implications that seem to underlie the vehemence of much of the revolutionary rhetoric surrounding hypertext:

Scholars are obliged to question common sense, interrogate its tacit presumptions and provoke new ways of looking at a familiar world.
. . .
Many quite nefarious ideologies pass for common sense.
. . .
If common sense sometimes preserves the social status quo, and that status quo sometimes treats unjust social hierarchies as natural, it makes good sense on such occasions to find ways of challenging common sense. Language that takes up this challenge can help point the way to a more socially just world.

In both Barthes's many subversions of clarity and Bakhtin's excoriation of monologism, one hears echoes of this idea that clarity works in the service of orthodoxy – of the self-evident, taken for granted, or commonsensical. This reification of orthodox structures of thought works to make readers passive consumers rather than active producers of these ideologies.

Hypermedia allow many of the characteristics that Barthes (1975: 4–5) posits as characterizing the **"triumphant plural"** of a writerly text:

Why is the writerly text of value? Because the goal of literary work (of literature as work) is to make the reader no longer a consumer, but a producer of the text.

...

Let us first posit the image of a **triumphant plural**, unimpoverished by any constraint of representation (of imitation). In this ideal text, the networks are many and interact, without any of them able to surpass the rest; this text is a galaxy of signifiers, not a structure of signifieds; it has no beginning; it is reversible; we gain access to it by several entrances, none of which can be authoritatively claimed to be the main one . . . the systems of meaning can take over this absolutely plural text, but their number is never closed, based as it is on the infinity of language.

Barthes's (again almost revolutionary) rhetoric of breaking out of the constraint of traditional representations echoes the canonical blasphemy and deconstructivist projects of the surrealists (Ray 1995). He seems to advocate practices that mirror surrealist experiments intended to form a revolutionary project by making unauthorized or "absurd" uses of canonical works to explode traditional structures of thought.

Hypermedia can in many ways be viewed as a tool or rhetorical methodology to engage in analogous "constructivist" projects that expand our notions of the limits of the possible. For writing/reading a hypermedia project often involves the use of absurd juxtapositions, fragments, and nonlinear linkages – many of the techniques posited (sometimes ecstatically) as the Holy Grail of escaping dominant structures of thought (Landow 1992, Deleuze and Guattari 1988, Ray 1995). Through hypermedia, we can move beyond "demythification" (in the Barthesian sense) to the creation of discourse outside or beyond the constraints of traditional rhetorical structures.

"Order needs justification, disorder does not . . ."

The natural state of things is *mess*.

...

Heteroglossia – Bakhtin's term for linguistic centrifugal forces and their products – continually translates the minute alterations and reevaluations of everyday life into new meanings and tones, which in sum and over time, always threaten the wholeness of any language. Language and all of culture are made by tiny and unsystematic alterations. Indeed, the wholeness of any cultural artifact is never "something given, but is always in essence posited – and at every moment . . . is opposed to the realities of heteroglossia" or other centrifugal forces. ("Discourse in the Novel," in Bakhtin 1981: 270)

As a result, wholeness is always a matter of work; it is not a gift, but a project. (Morson and Emerson 1990: 30; italics in original)

The finalized works that we create as part of the tropics of academic argumentation and practices of academic publishing often belie the life-history – the ongoing dialogues that are monologized within a system that rewards individual accomplishment in an often competitive and sometimes confrontational atmosphere. Writing practices that are perhaps more representative of the development of ideas before, during, and after their publication might include the extensive cross-referentiality and openings provided by hypermedia (as well as the possibility of their continual transformation via linking, as in the World Wide Web). The inclusion of contradictory voices or even the internal contradictions of a "single" author, can reflect the fragments and nuances of the internal and external dialogues with past and future interlocutors.

Interlude: "The Word with a Loophole" (Morson and Emerson 1990:159) Or, Crafting "Crafting *Crafting Cosmos*"

The challenge I face in **Part 3** is how to present, in the traditional academic format of a text-based narrative, an argument that centers on the notion that certain forms of knowledge construction and deconstruction can best (and perhaps *only*) be expressed through multiple media and hypermedia (compare Tringham 1998). This "translation" requires that I engage in a sort of reverse flow of media inventions – of visual idioms and ways of reading – by integrating or re-creating in book form some of the features of reading/writing hypermedia. Inherent in the original project is an emphasis on the integration and equalization of text, images, and sound. Due to the nature of book publication, the reprioritization of text cannot be avoided. However, where possible, I will attempt to represent some of the aspects of hypermedia – the modes of navigation, pathways, gateways, and juxtapositions that allow for the creation of a multiplicity of dialogues in the quest for a triumphant plural (figures 4.1–4.20).

Part 3: *Crafting Cosmos*

Crafting Cosmos is an exploration of how the unique aspects of hypermedia and hypertext allow connections to be made among diverse bodies and types of information – of how to represent the many avenues through which we come to understand and interpret past societies and their use of material culture in creating and re-

creating society – and of how we might then embody or humanize
our interpretations to convey the significance of human agency.
Throughout this project, I grapple with how to compose hypermedia
to encourage the reader/writer to explore nontraditional expressions
of academic arguments that reflect both their nonlinear, often unme-
thodical genesis, and the many sources of inspiration, imagination,
and accident that generate the interpretations that are so often
monologized in academic prose. I am primarily concerned with how
to visualize, exemplify, and even embody the abstract arguments we
make about past societies. If culture only exists in its enactment, then
through what processes do we reconstruct or "reenact" narratives of
the past?

The central metaphor of "crafting" and the choice of focusing on
the crafters of material culture as agents who both re-created and
created Maya society during the Late to Terminal Classic period (AD
600–1000) has roots (or rhizomes) in my ongoing dialogue with a
household site I excavated in the Ulúa Valley, Honduras. It began with
a rather monologized site report (well, actually it began with the
cacophony that is an archaeological excavation, which was then
monologized into a site report), in which I exhaustively described the
excavations, characterized and catalogued the amounts and kinds of
artifacts and architecture found, and interpreted the activities carried
out at the household level (Lopiparo 1994). I methodically enumer-
ated the multiple lines of evidence indicating that this household site
was the locus of small-scale ceramic production, and have argued that
it and contemporary sites in the valley have extensive evidence suggesting that household level production of fine-paste ceramics was
ubiquitous, spanning the period of transition between the Late and
Terminal Classic – a period hypothesized to be so tumultuous to
Maya sociopolitical and economic structures that it bears the name
"The Classic Maya Collapse" (Lopiparo 2001, Lopiparo, Joyce and
Hendon 2000). I have subsequently focused on the significance of
continuous, dispersed, and widespread participation in the production of shared material culture during this period, especially given
that the Ulúa Valley not only showed no evidence of a breakdown
of sociopolitical and economic structures, but continued to flourish
during the Terminal Classic, with a continued pattern of fairly dispersed household settlements concurrent with the development of its
largest center at Cerro Palenque (Hendon and Lopiparo in press,
R. Joyce 1991).

The common dichotomization between craft specialization and
household production (Clark and Parry 1990, Costin 1991) – with its

implication that domestic production was for personal use, while craft production was an industry linked to a larger economic superstructure – necessarily ties together increased "complexity," as indicated primarily by settlement centralization, with hierarchy, in the form of an assumption of centralized control of production activities and their products. Interpretations of Classic Maya societies commonly assert models of overarching, centralized sociopolitical structures that are presumed to control the production of material culture – and hence not only the production of knowledge about identity and affiliation, but the very distribution of resources and power that such a control of ideas implies. Artifactual and compositional evidence for localized production and exchange (for example, evidence for dispersed production and consumption of Terminal Classic fine-paste ceramics, often characterized as "elite" wares) seems to call into question the by now "commonsensical" correlation of centralization with economic hierarchy. Through an agency-focused reconstruction of microscale processes of organization of ceramic production, and of the internal and external relationships of ceramic producers and their products, we can consider both the independent identity of domestic groups as cultural producers – as well as their identification with larger groups, and mutual participation in – and therefore constitution of – larger socioeconomic structures (compare Tringham 1996).

"Households with faces" (Tringham 1991)

But how can we envision and embody this connection between "Crafting . . ." – the production activities of human agents at the microscale of the household – and "Constitution . . ." – the enactment and creation of larger-scale social structures?

The inspiration for the metaphor I use in *Crafting Cosmos* began as I imagined how an individual dialogically enacts culture – the inherited notions of utility, aesthetics, economics, etc. – through the creation of and interaction with material culture. How does an artifact – as a unique utterance in every new situation into which it enters – participate in the flow of the ongoing dialogue of social memory? I began to envision in three dimensions a set of features that included a series of shallow pits that I believe were used for processing clay, a small hearth in which ceramics were fired, and a specialized midden that included figurine and vessel molds – all adjacent to a wattle-and-daub structure that contained a full range of artifacts characterizing general domestic activities – i.e., a house. Then people began to populate this place – a parent and child (OK, a mother and daughter), the mother preparing the clay and pressing it into the mold of a figurine of a *viejo*, while telling the child the story of how their ancestors first made this place. The entrance of this artifact into the flow of time, as a mnemonic for notions of identity, place, and continuity, exemplified in microcosm what households do to produce and reproduce culture in the processes of producing and reproducing themselves. Gillespie's (2000b) discussion of "Maya nested houses" and household rituals as the enactment of the universe in microcosm in many ways formed the grounding metaphor for *Crafting Cosmos* – for when we formulate this construction backwards, the universe is the house in macrocosm (Gillespie 2000b: 159). One does not determine the other, but rather they only exist in dialogue with each other.

"The medium is the message" (McLuhan 1994:7)

While *Crafting Cosmos* is intended to be nonlinear, it does very prominently interweave the central themes discussed in this chapter through the structure of the project and navigation itself. And, again, I am aware of the irony that my post-structuralist argument is made in the structure of my project – on the other hand it is the reader/writer that creates their own dialogical understanding through navigating and interacting with the fragments and connections assembled (and disassembled and reassembled) in each potentially unique "reading" of the hypermedia project. Because of the fundamental role of material culture in archaeologists' narrativization of the past, it is also crucial to foreground – or at least equalize – not only the visual, but also other channels and sources of inspiration for our interpretations. (Sound, music, multiple voices, movement, and animation are all used in the project to represent and embody human agents in the past.)

How the strands of my argument are interwoven can be approached through the three metaphors for navigating *Crafting Cosmos*. The first navigational element of the project is time, and is based on the cyclical notions of time that are frequently described as being inherent in Classic Maya calendrics. In these conceptions of time, past and present were integrated in a complex web of relations mediated by the ancestors, who were called upon to intervene in matters of daily and state life. Their deeds were integral to claims of authority and prosperity. A cyclical conception of time, frequently associated with ancestor worship, has been argued to be a central prin-

ciple of Classic Maya cosmology, appearing in archaeological contexts
from the scale of state legitimation of rulership in Classic Maya stelae
to the organization of households.

It is in this interpenetration of past and present that *Crafting
Cosmos* draws parallels between how Classic Maya societies created
meaning in *their* present through the ongoing dialogic (re)creation of
social memory – particularly through the creation and interaction
with material culture – and how archaeologists, often in dialogue with
this same material culture, reconstruct meaning in the past and create
meaning in their present. Thus it is through the navigation of time,
represented in the icon of the Maya calendar in *Crafting Cosmos*, that
one can explore parallels between archaeologists' interpretations of
how the Maya interwove past and present, and how archaeologists
partake in the same project. Each major node of the project has a past
and present aspect to illustrate the parallels between how the ancient
Maya crafted their cosmos through daily practices, and how we as
archaeologists craft our present through the practices of archaeology
and the representations, interpretations, and narrativizations of
material culture.

The second strand of this argument, represented by four crafts-
people in the corners of the navigation page (Scribe, Weaver, Sculptor, and Cultivator), focuses specifically on how people as crafters
create their own universe through daily practices, and how these
understandings are embedded in material culture. As a case study, I
draw on my ongoing investigations of domestic production during
the Late to Terminal Classic transition in the Ulúa Valley, and thus
focus first on the household, and then consider how these practices
interrelate with those at higher levels of organization and aggregation.
I consider craft production both from an economic and utilitarian
perspective – how people provide for the subsistence and continuity
of their societies and interact with other corporate groups – and also
from the standpoint of the ideational role that material culture plays
in the demarcation and continuation of the household group. Both
household industry as the physical manifestation of the "(re)produc-
tion" of the domestic group, and household ritual, as the entry of
that material culture into an active role in claiming and maintaining
group identity, productivity, and continuity, include practices that
metaphorically and literally are acts of creation and means of embodying, embedding, and inscribing ideals and meanings. These activities
are also those which provide some of our most abundant resources
as archaeologists. By considering material culture as forming part of
living dialogues in which ideas are inscribed by their crafters and

received and negotiated by those who interact with them, we can begin to visualize the ways that social memory is embodied, propagated, and negotiated by social agents – how the creation of these "objects" becomes an essential link in the dialogic creation of subjects (and society, as their intersubjective social relations).

Crafters as social agents intersect with the time navigation in an explicitly self-reflexive, epistemological thread of the project, which includes multiple investigations:

1   paralleling our role as scribes to those of Classic Maya scribes as crafters of the present, through the production and inscription of official (pre)histories;
2   paralleling the importance of weavers and the metaphoric act of weaving in shaping identity, to the practices of archaeologists weaving together diverse strands of information (ethnographic, oral historic, linguistic, ethnohistoric, glyphic, stylistic, artistic, archaeological) to define what *is* "Maya";
3   considering the role of sculptors (as one example of representational artists – particularly on the level of small-scale production) in embodying and embedding ideals of personhood in permanent media as a means of propagating social memory – in relation to theoretical arguments about how structuration "works" (for example, through a narrative animation of a parent telling a story to a child while modeling a figurine); and finally,
4   paralleling the fundamental but oft-ignored importance of "cultivators" (as a general metaphor for providers/feeders/caregivers) in providing the basic necessities and foundations for the development of one's ideas of personhood, identity, and society to the role of the "cultivators" of archaeological data (see chapter 2) as providing the sustenance/foundations/basic necessities from which archaeologists develop their conceptions and ideas of both prehistoric and modern peoples [the typically gendered notions of "women's work," for example, of women as feeders/providers of sustenance, is emphasized here – particularly in reference to "archaeological housework" (after Gero 1985)].

The third and probably most fundamental focus of the underlying argument concerns how hypermedia can be used to visualize and express the concepts of structuration and practice theories – to represent the structure–agency dialectic. This relationship is conceptualized metaphorically through the Maya symbol of the world tree, which represents the tripartite division of the Maya universe, with the upperworld (the realm of supernatural beings associated with nature and the creation of the earthly world) representing "structure," the earthly world (the realm of humans) representing "agency/practices," and the underworld (the realm of the ancestors) representing the "traditions," roots, and specific histories which constrain and define the circumstances and choices of agents. The tree itself is an *axis mundi* to connect these levels of the universe, their interactions representing the dialectical processes of structuration (see figures 4.1–4.4).

Again there is a past/present aspect to the world trees, two past and two present. World Tree Past 1 explores the interpretation of the meaning of the Classic Maya symbol itself, with an explanation of the tripartite division – less as a division than as an assertion of human agency in the creation of polity and society. World Tree Past 2 explores the nested levels of ancient ritual through which aspects of this world tree were brought into practice as the *axis mundi* that allowed interaction and communication among the different levels. Specifically, I explore the relationship between household and state ritual and their common basis for legitimation and continuity in the realm of ancestors. World Tree Present 3 focuses on the practices of archaeology itself (particularly household archaeology), with excavations and data from sites in the Ulúa Valley serving as the roots or fundaments for the interpretations of household activities or small-scale practices that are in turn utilized to make statements about social organization. World Tree Present 4 explicitly addresses the theoretical basis for the structure and the arguments made in the project – of how the practices of social agents produce, reproduce, and negotiate structures of society within the constraints of their specific histories. Each of these world trees serves both as its own internal dialogue and in conjunction and interaction with the other world trees. Thus connections can be made "vertically" among the nested levels of the trees and "horizontally" (or perhaps rhizomically) among the trees themselves – and among the trees and the crafters.

So after setting up this tangled infrastructure of nodes and pathways, I was faced with the challenge of operationalizing my rhetoric, of crafting content and connections in the creation of hypermedia that would be truly plural in their possibilities for unique readings and creation of new juxtapositions between textual and nontextual media. It was also my goal to juxtapose the many different sources that archaeologists draw on in their reconstructions and narrativizations of the past.

One central issue was the reinstatement of people into my arguments emphasizing the importance of human agency. Ironically, this was probably the most difficult aspect of the project because of the inherent difficulties of representation. After many failed attempts at animating people, I was inspired by Patricia Amlin's movie of *The Popol Vuh* made by animating figures from Classic Maya polychrome vessels. The solution of using representations created by "the represented" seemed to add other voices – which in turn needed to be contextualized in terms of who created these vessels, for what purpose, who was excluded, etc. As a counterbalance to the risk of reifying a Pan-Maya stylistic identity by mixing and matching pots from different contexts, *Crafting Cosmos* incorporates many links to the study of localized production of pottery and localized production of identity through material culture.

And so, leaving no loophole unlinked, I decided to pursue this avenue by making figures from polychrome vessels "speak" using animated quotes from ethnohistoric and ethnographic sources. These narrations of course fire up another round of action and retraction because they too are from a mixture of time periods and areas – which then allows another opening for the exploration of how archaeologists use these and similar sources in more traditional academic writing to narrativize the past. The excerpts are intended to resonate with the ideas that are being expressed in the nodes (including ideas about crafting, creation, production, memory, ancestors), creating juxtapositions that both implicitly include interpretations of the meanings of these utterances to the original speakers or writers of the narratives, and of their uses in archaeologists' writing of the past (see figures 4.5–4.15).

But the stories aren't the only means of making connections among traditionally disparate types of knowledge. The second major mechanism or avenue of "hyperness" that I focused on developing was hypertext links – for which even rhizomes are perhaps too orderly a metaphor. My intention is to create a veritable underground maze that connects even the most disparate of nodes in the project (for example, data on *incensario* fragments to stories about burning offerings, or discussions about ideological hegemony to stela inscriptions, or subfloor burials linked to → ancestors → household ritual → figurines → paper on the inscription of ideas in material culture → sculptor . . .). The possibilities for new connections and juxtapositions, while limited to the universe of the project (which was not designed as a website), is potentially unique for each reading/writing of the project, with readers/writers engaging in the dialogues and connections that most interest them. I hope to adapt this project for the Web, in order to allow possibilities for the addition of feedback, responses, discussions, and external links, and also to allow for the expansion, response, and modification of the universe of the site itself.[8]

The hypertext links in *Crafting Cosmos* are hidden until the cursor passes over them, which both introduces the element of chance in determining which connections the readers/writers will find and make, but also allows for them to look for and follow whatever part of the page engages their attention – and therefore to be aware of what and where they hope to find connections and what strands of thought they want to pursue. One concession that I made against my inherent and perhaps diabolical urge to force people to get lost (which in some ways goes hand-in-hand with hiddenness) is to create a tiny (and also hidden) hypertext back arrow, so you can always return to where you came from via a hypertext link. I have become convinced that not to do so would violate some inherent social contract of interactivity in the "civilized" world (a feature that interestingly would be difficult if not impossible to subvert in a Web version, thanks to the new ways of "reading" imposed by Web browsers).

I also conceded – though also halfheartedly *and* in my own not-so-helpful way – to a "Help" section, which is intended to make more transparent my ideas, intentions, and elaborate schemes behind the creation and construction of *Crafting Cosmos*. And, in fact, it reads like a condensed and disjointed version of this exegesis (which will probably appear in some form in future incarnations of the project). The (not-so-) HELP (-ful) section follows two interleaved trains of thought, titled "Method to the Madness" and "Lost and Found." The first introduces the theoretical underpinnings and agendas behind the project, while the second introduces the means of navigating the site and reasons for installing these particular navigation systems.

Fundamental to the project are (potentially infinitely expandable) nodes to present information about my (and perhaps others') ongoing excavations in the Ulúa Valley, as the "food" or fundaments from which the project grows (see figures 4.16–4.20). From databases about materials, to images, photos, maps, and drawings, to Harris matrices, to reconstructions and interpretations of households and activities, the many levels of archaeological inference are being documented in an interactive, textual and visual (and even auditory and video) format. These in turn are linked through many and multivalent paths to arguments about social processes and social structures, while being situated in the self-reflexive dialogues about the processes and projects of knowledge construction – dialogues in which this is just one utterance.

The underground man is always trying to elude the power of the other to define him and always trying to prevent any "finalized" image of himself from fixing. He therefore continually polemicizes with the impression his words might make, and seems to mock and retract what he has said before he has finished saying it. He even retracts his own tendency to retraction, and ridicules in advance even his tendency to use preemptive double-voiced discourse. It is as if he understood all possible analyses of himself . . . and was trying to disarm them, to stun the analysts before the words were out of their mouths. (Morson and Emerson 1990: 159–60)

4.1

4.2

Figures 4.1–4.4 *A sample reading of* Crafting Cosmos. *The pointing hand shows the links selected by the reader (in this case, Jeanne Lopiparo). These screens demonstrate navigation using the world tree metaphor*

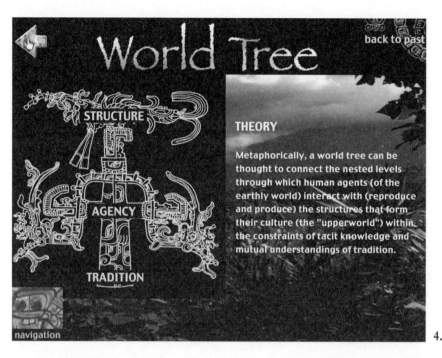

World Tree

back to past

STRUCTURE

AGENCY

TRADITION

THEORY

Metaphorically, a world tree can be thought to connect the nested levels through which human agents (of the earthly world) interact with (reproduce and produce) the structures that form their culture (the "upperworld") within the constraints of tacit knowledge and mutual understandings of tradition.

navigation

4.3

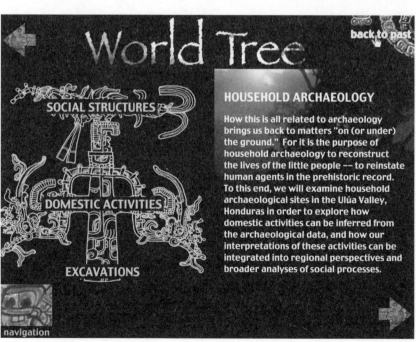

World Tree

back to past

SOCIAL STRUCTURES

DOMESTIC ACTIVITIES

EXCAVATIONS

HOUSEHOLD ARCHAEOLOGY

How this is all related to archaeology brings us back to matters "on (or under) the ground." For it is the purpose of household archaeology to reconstruct the lives of the little people -- to reinstate human agents in the prehistoric record. To this end, we will examine household archaeological sites in the Ulúa Valley, Honduras in order to explore how domestic activities can be inferred from the archaeological data, and how our interpretations of these activities can be integrated into regional perspectives and broader analyses of social processes.

navigation

4.4

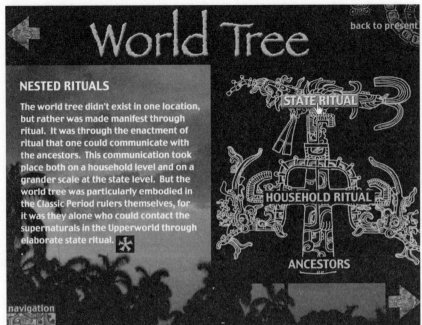

World Tree

back to present

NESTED RITUALS

The world tree didn't exist in one location, but rather was made manifest through ritual. It was through the enactment of ritual that one could communicate with the ancestors. This communication took place both on a household level and on a grander scale at the state level. But the world tree was particularly embodied in the Classic Period rulers themselves, for it was they alone who could contact the supernaturals in the Upperworld through elaborate state ritual.

STATE RITUAL

HOUSEHOLD RITUAL

ANCESTORS

navigation

4.5

Jaguar Night, Mahucutah, and True Jaguar were our first grandfathers, Jaguar Quitze,

STATE RITUAL

4.6

Figures 4.5–4.15 *This section of the reading explores the juxtapositions of revoiced utterances in heteroglossic dialogues*

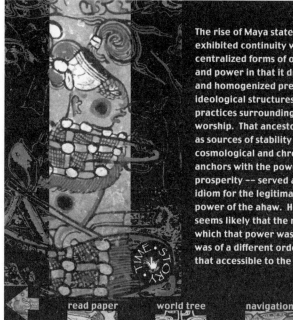

The rise of Maya statehood exhibited continuity with less centralized forms of organization and power in that it drew on and homogenized preexisting ideological structures and ritual practices surrounding ancestor worship. That ancestors stood as sources of stability -- as cosmological and chronological anchors with the power to ensure prosperity -- served as a powerful idiom for the legitimacy of the power of the ahaw. However it seems likely that the realm in which that power was enacted was of a different order than that accessible to the masses.

read paper   world tree   navigation

4.7

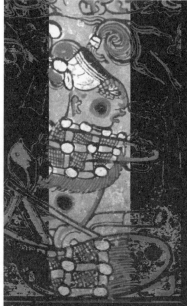

And this was the beginning and growth of the Quiché, when the Lord Plumed Serpent made the signs of greatness. His face was not forgotten by his grandsons and sons. He didn't do these things just so there would be one single lord, a being of genius, but they had the effect of humbling all the tribes when he did them. It was just his way of revealing himself, but because of it he became the sole head of the tribes

....

And so he left signs and sayings for the next generation. They achieved splendor and majesty, and they, too, begot sons, making the sons still more populous.... They begot another generation of lords.

◄ HIDE

Tedlock, Dennis 1985 *Popol Vuh: The Maya Book of the Dawn of Life.* New York: Simon & Schuster, Inc. 212-3.

4.8

Within this realm there is a distinct but often ignored differentiation between types of supernaturals. As Gossen and Leventhal note: "The picture of the ancient Maya religion continues to become complex and clouded when one turns to the center and identifies the existence not only of ancestor worship but also the worship of a series of deities tied to the natural world." Perhaps it was the ability to interact with the supernatural realm of creation itself that was the quality or claim of legitimacy which differentiated and distanced the ahaw lineages from the ancestors of the masses, and initiated the verticalization or homogenization of ritual practices that signaled the ideological allegiance of local groups to a higher order of organization -- to a higher order of power.

Within the ancient world, the city centers were, at an earlier time, a part of the periphery. They were single family household groups that grew and gradually became the focal points of cities for numerous reasons not to be examined here. The center, therefore, is the periphery transformed, writ large, and formalized. Ancestor worship becomes structured and the animal souls, spooks, and natural deities of the periphery become formalized into a state religion.

read paper　　　world tree　　　navigation

4.9

ANCESTORS

Release their spirits and send them to us.

4.10

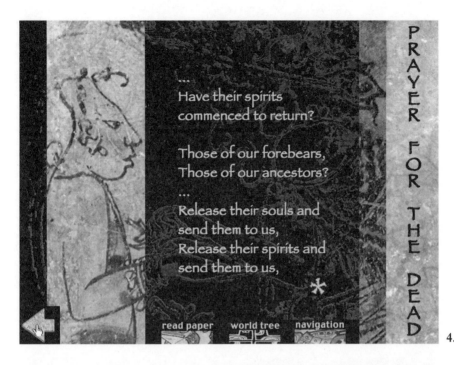

...
Have their spirits
commenced to return?

Those of our forebears,
Those of our ancestors?

...
Release their souls and
send them to us,
Release their spirits and
send them to us,

*

read paper   world tree   navigation

PRAYER FOR THE DEAD

4.11

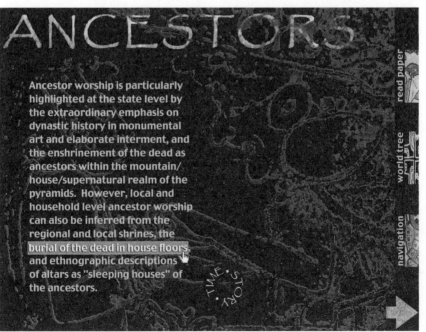

ANCESTORS

Ancestor worship is particularly
highlighted at the state level by
the extraordinary emphasis on
dynastic history in monumental
art and elaborate interment, and
the enshrinement of the dead as
ancestors within the mountain/
house/supernatural realm of the
pyramids. However, local and
household level ancestor worship
can also be inferred from the
regional and local shrines, the
burial of the dead in house floors,
and ethnographic descriptions
of altars as "sleeping houses" of
the ancestors.

read paper

world tree

navigation

TIME · STORY

4.12

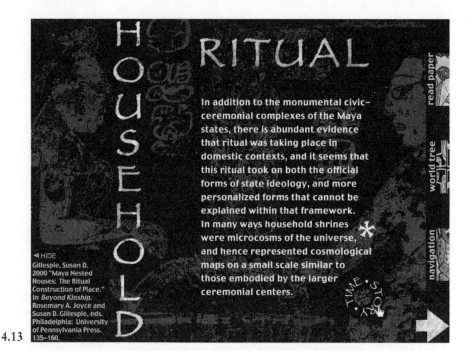

HOUSEHOLD RITUAL

In addition to the monumental civic–ceremonial complexes of the Maya states, there is abundant evidence that ritual was taking place in domestic contexts, and it seems that this ritual took on both the official forms of state ideology, and more personalized forms that cannot be explained within that framework. In many ways household shrines were microcosms of the universe, and hence represented cosmological maps on a small scale similar to those embodied by the larger ceremonial centers.

read paper

world tree

navigation

TIME · STOP · BY

◄ HIDE

Gillespie, Susan D. 2000 "Maya Nested Houses: The Ritual Construction of Place." In *Beyond Kinship*. Rosemary A. Joyce and Susan D. Gillespie, eds. Philadelphia: University of Pennsylvania Press. 135–160.

4.13

SHRINE PRAYER

If there is our mother,
our father

who unites words behind
our legs our arms;

go to the place the sun comes
from, to the place the sun falls

four corners of the sky,
four corners of the earth.

Here is the offering
for the blessing, the favor

for our house,
for our land....

◄ HIDE

EXCERPTED FROM "SHRINE PRAYER":
Tedlock, Barbara 1992 *Time and the Highland Maya*, Revised Edition. Albuquerque: University of New Mexico Press. 241–3.

4.14

But how might this heterogeneity be read in the archaeological record? While there are always archaeological materials that are labeled generically as evidence of ritual (as a residual category for "no discernible utilitarian function"), there are also plenty of instances in which ritual can be reasonably inferred -- such as careful arrangements and burials of figurines (and of course humans), caches, household altars, and objects, such as incensarios, which ethnographically and ethnohistorically have exclusive and well-documented ritual uses.

Many of these artifacts cannot necessarily be made sense of within the framework of official religion. It is only by referencing the heterogeneous practices encountered by the Spanish, that many of these artifacts begin to "make sense" outside the commonly accepted homogeneous framework of Classic Maya religion.

We do not have much archaeological evidence for the domestic remains of those mainland agriculturalists that the Spaniards found so ubiquitous, living in simple houses near their fields and worshipping their gods in the woods and in caves....

read paper

world tree

navigation

4.15

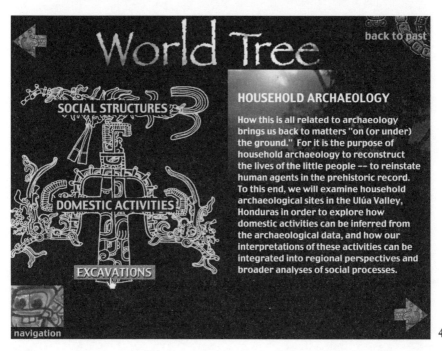

4.16

Figures 4.16–4.20 Crafting Cosmos *grows from the household archaeology of the roots of Classic Maya Society*

EXCAVATIONS

GULF OF HONDURAS

100 m

OMOA MOUNTAINS

100 m

CHAMELECON RIVER

ULÚA RIVER

Curruste

ULÚA VALLEY HONDURAS

Cerro Palenque

Travesía

Campo de los Muertos

Xacamaya

0   5   10 km

As the bases for our explorations of social processes from the bottom up, we will examine the excavations of household sites in the Ulúa Valley, Honduras. The goals of my research in the valley include investigating how the production and uses of material culture both reflected and shaped the structures of society -- how people created their world in everyday life and constructed their identities, affiliations, communities, and polities within the world through their social practices, rather than how a disembodied "civilization" determined the domestic, socioeconomic, and political roles of a subjugated people.

navigation   world tree   read paper

4.17

EXCAVATIONS

This satellite photo shows the central alluvium of the Ulúa Valley, including the study area of the Proyecto Arqueológico Clásico Terminal. The broad ribbon of the Ulúa River highlights the possible networks of internal and external relationships among these sites, as well as the potential social and economic significance of their location on the fertile floodplain just downriver from Cerro Palenque, the largest center in the valley during the Terminal Classic period. Sites in the central alluvium have an architecture distinct from the cobble mounded sites of the surrounding hills. They feature primarily small wattle–and–daub structures built on top of broad, ovoid earthen rises (called "lomas"), that were built up over time and had continuous occupation from the Late to Terminal Classic (and in some cases dating back thousands of years to the Early Formative).

P.A.C.T. STUDY AREA

Cerro Palenque

navigation   world tree   read paper

4.18

EXCAVATIONS

PROYECTO ARQUEOLÓGICO
CLÁSICO TERMINAL

RESEARCH OBJECTIVES

ANTHROPOLOGICAL CONTEXT

PROJECT BACKGROUND

DISCUSSION

CR-381

CR-80

CR-103

CR-132

2km

4.19

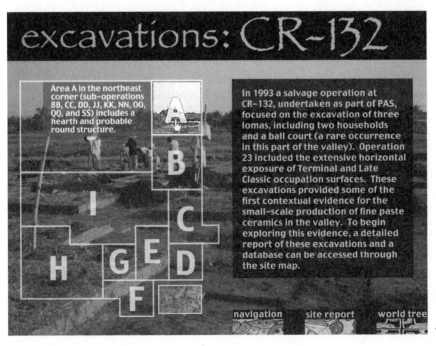

excavations: CR-132

Area A in the northeast corner (sub-operations BB, CC, DD, JJ, KK, NN, OO, QQ, and SS) includes a hearth and probable round structure.

A

B

I

C

H G E D

F

In 1993 a salvage operation at CR-132, undertaken as part of PAS, focused on the excavation of three lomas, including two households and a ball court (a rare occurrence in this part of the valley). Operation 23 included the extensive horizontal exposure of Terminal and Late Classic occupation surfaces. These excavations provided some of the first contextual evidence for the small-scale production of fine paste ceramics in the valley. To begin exploring this evidence, a detailed report of these excavations and a database can be accessed through the site map.

navigation   site report   world tree

4.20

5

Voices Carry Outside
the Discipline

Writing Sister Stories

Bakhtin argued that narrative genres (which he recognized as including the humanities and human, or social, sciences) involve the creation of dialogues between an author and an other, whose status is not that of an object of study but of another subject (Todorov 1984: 22–4). He distinguished such texts from those produced by the sciences, in which the discursive object remained an object, and texts attained the form of a monologue on these objects (Todorov 1984: 17–22, 80–5). Archaeology famously straddles the division between humanities and sciences, so it is perhaps not surprising that Bakhtin's proposals imply anomalous status for archaeology no matter which position it adopts.

Archaeology begins with a confrontation with something material that exists independently of the archaeologist. The archaeologist can apparently adopt the perspective of the scientist, creating monologues in which this material stands as an object. But in Bakhtin's philosophy, such apparent monologic perspective is illusory, since the author of the text cannot completely close off the meaning of the things he or she treats as objects of study (Todorov 1984: 107). The monologic perspective sees the material as *requiring* the scientist-author for completion, for endowment of meaning. This conceit can be sustained in sciences whose objects are without apparent creators, but is completely untenable in disciplines where it is obvious from the outset that other thinking actors have intervened in the production of the material under consideration. An archaeologist may consider his or her production of meaning as independent of any past meanings, or of unknown and unknowable relationship to past meanings, but he or she begins with the knowledge that the material of past human experience was already endowed with meaning by others. Archaeologists cannot escape the knowledge that they do not complete and encompass the material they study by making it the object of their regard (compare Mignolo 1995: 1–25). Even if they choose not to engage the problematics of the other subjects in the past for whom archaeological materials figured as meaningful, they cannot *deny* their former existence.

Increasingly, in fact, archaeologists are forced to acknowledge the intersubjectivity of even the most apparently objective relations they construct to archaeological material, by the intervention in the present of others who are not academics in discourses about such things (see, for example, Layton 1989a, 1989b, Leone and Preucel 1992, Lowenthal 1990, Murray 1993, Schmidt and Patterson 1995, Wylie 1992b, 1995, 1996). While past subjects may not be able to speak up to contradict the present archaeologist, *other* others increasingly do so. The legitimate status of the voices of other stakeholders has become a widely accepted, although not uncontested, fact, embodied, for example, in revisions to fundamental concepts of the Society for American Archaeology Code of Ethics (Lynott and Wylie 1995, Wylie 1996; see also R. Joyce 1999a).

No archaeological narrative can ever be convincingly presented as closed, except by invoking authority over archaeological material that would require it to be completely objective, rather than (as it is) the matter of intersubjectivity through time. This is not a claim for complete relativism. Recursive attention to features or their previously unregarded variation can always permit new, materially responsible narratives, that through their accumulation result in denser, less deterministic, and hence more realistic stories about the past. The openness of narrative is something to be celebrated, not something to be feared; and yet, the failure to achieve closure is the primary criticism that threatens attempts to open up archaeological storytelling. Here I turn to *Sister Stories* (Joyce, Guyer, and Joyce 2000), a hypertext narrative, to examine the negotiation of meaning in which archaeology increasingly must engage.

Sister Stories was arrived at through a collaboration between myself, Michael Joyce (my brother), and Carolyn Guyer (my sister-in-law), the latter two writers and theorists of hypertext fiction (Guyer 1992, 1996, Guyer and Petry 1991, M. Joyce 1995, 2000). The original content for *Sister Stories* was drawn from the *Florentine Codex*, a multivolume work compiled by the sixteenth-century Spanish Franciscan friar, Bernardino de Sahagún (see Edmonson 1974, Klor de Alva, Nicholson and Quiñones Keber 1988, Mignolo 1995: 186–216). I selected sections from the *Florentine Codex*, drawing primarily on a modern edition with side-by-side publication of English

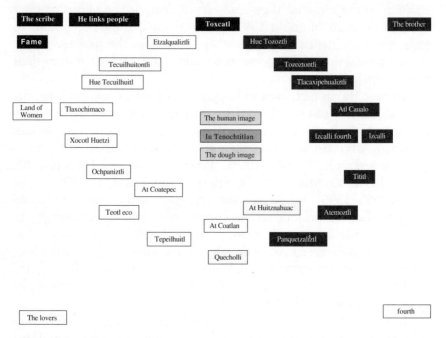

Figure 5.1 *The original opening screen of* Sister Stories, *showing the original iconic layout of the top level of spaces*

translation by A. J. O. Anderson and Charles Dibble, opposite Nahuatl text edited by the same authorities (Sahagún 1950–82).

I presented this text to my collaborators in an iconic form (figure 5.1, http://www.nyupress.nyu.edu/sisterstories/feathered.fir/ ss.circlemap.html), created using *Storyspace*, that placed selected text in spatial locations intended to recall the geographic and temporal contexts with which it was linked for Nahuatl speakers in sixteenth-century Mexico. My collaborators wrote in and around this text, bringing to it their own experiences and attempts to understand the content as I structured it and conveyed it from Sahagún, who structured and conveyed it from a body of noble, male speakers after the fall of the Mexica state to the Spanish conquistadors. I then added my own text, written from my standpoint as a scholar of related Central American cultures called on to teach about the Mexica, or Aztecs, to an increasingly diverse student body, many of whom bring to these texts their own historical concerns with what they feel is their national cultural heritage. The final *Storyspace* work consisted of 313 spaces, integrated by 1,811 links and 603 paths, containing 40,423 words[9] (about two-thirds the length of the book you are reading).

The initial universe I presented to my collaborators was an abstract from an already fragmented original. Sahagún's own texts were multiple, beginning around 1547 with a first approximation published as the *Primeros Memoriales* (Sahagún 1993) in which the balance of images and texts was reversed, with brief captions as glosses on pictures. Although the *Florentine Codex* as assembled around 1569 was presented as a coherent work, Sahagún dispersed texts elicited at multiple times and in different ways across multiple volumes, according to a medieval European scheme of universal encyclopediac knowledge (Mignolo 1995: 192–9). The texts, as archaeological materials, are irreducibly intersubjective dialogues. "Decades of Mexica informants responding to the old Franciscan Sahagún's proto-ethnographies successively learned from these questions themselves how to tell him the stories in the forms his culture could hear" (M. Joyce 2000). While *Sister Stories* is obviously multivocal, it is not without structure. It serves as a model of one way archaeological storytelling could acknowledge the existence of multiple stakeholders without losing sight of our communal concern with responsibility about the past (R. Joyce 1998b).

Third Dialogue: Telling Sister Stories

Rosemary A. Joyce, Carolyn Guyer, and Michael Joyce[10]

Background for *Sister Stories*

Among the Mexica, "the good scribe," it is said in the *Codex Florentino*, "knew very well the genealogies of the lords" and of him it was said, "He links the people well; he places them in order."

Sister stories know a different order, they link not by placing but by finding places within which to be. They know very well what, in *The Making of Americans*, Gertrude Stein called "all the kinds of ways there can be seen to be kinds of men and women." Hypertext, a linking technology, tells of different orders. Hyperfiction artists Carolyn Guyer and Michael Joyce together with archaeologist Rosemary Joyce (Michael's sister) ⟨. . .⟩ created this work with the hope that "in a history of many men and women," as Stein says, "sometimes there will be a history of every one."

For background specific to Aztec culture, click here

Rosemary

Sister Stories is not an introduction to Aztec society. It deliberately invites you to read Nahuatl texts in English translation to arrive at your own sense of what these materials imply, evoke, hint at. Disorientation is the best kind of response one can have to the prospect of trying to make sense of a culture, now 500 years in the past, that grew from roots utterly distinct from Europe, Asia, and Africa.

But I don't want you to be discouraged. I have provided notes – my own views, sometimes those of others – on Aztec society in general, and on topics you may find difficult in particular. I would hope you will defer reading these for now; they will often be available from the Aztec readings in this work, along paths bearing my name [use the Question Mark Tool to see which links these are]. But if you think some initial commentary will help, this is a place to start.

– Rosemary Joyce

To gather More Background, click here

What I would like

It would be easy to either dismiss or romanticize the lives of Aztec women. When I teach this material, I have learned to place certain topics out of bounds for student papers. The list has been short: human sacrifice, cannibalism, bloodletting. I have begun to wish I could justify adding women to the list of topics too complex for a single semester's worth of thought.

Reading the authorities, my students inevitably find that Aztec women led lives full of oppression. I do not recognize these patterns. I want to recover another reading from these texts, in which women's lives were celebrated from before birth and after death.

To accept this alternative, though, I find I have to lead my students straight through the very topics I am reluctant to have them write about, and others less exotic but equally unintelligible: the value of labor, the comfort of having a defined place in a family, and the pervasive presence of the sacred in the everyday.

pattern forming

http://www.nyupress.nyu.edu/sisterstories/tecuilhuitontli/
pattern.forming.html

It was always that she went out, and then landed where they kept
her in. It wasn't just that she was expected to bear children and
keep the blood moving. That too of course. But there are all those
other children. The ones that tumble and screech beneath the
young bride's feet, under her arms, around her shoulders as she
sits, a welcoming turbulence, an initiation. What kind of aunt will
you be?

   She learned all their stories, memorizing because she hadn't the
ease of lived memory. Who was born when, which of the men were
most respected, which of the women most cherished, who liked
mashed potatoes and who couldn't stand raisins. She studied,
became the scholar and receptacle of their lives.

Song of Ayopechtli

> Somewhere
> Somewhere in Ayopechtli's home
> she lies adorned with necklace jewels
> giving birth
> ⟨. . .⟩
> Bestir yourself, be sent
> Bestir yourself, jewel child
> Bestir yourself

Florentine Codex II, Appendix

Birth

"And when the baby was born, they read the day signs. They
summoned the diviner, they told him the instant it had arrived, the
instant it had been born. Then he looked at, he opened the
writings. The diviner studied the day signs. . . . Then he chose a
good day, not just the fourth day hence, that it be bathed. He still
skipped; he sought a good day, or a good one of its companions
which governed there."

(*Florentine Codex* VI, ch. 36; fig. 28)

Aztec Drawings Tour

http://www.nyupress.org/sisterstories/help/illus.index.html

Cuicalli

http://www.nyupress.org/sisterstories/calpulli/calpulli.html

"Cuicalli: there were the masters of the youths and the rulers of
the youths, established in order to oversee what was by way of
work. And every day, when the sun had already set, they turned
their attention to dances. They went quite naked. So they went to
the house of songs; so they danced with song, proceeding with,
about their necks, only a cape made like a net. They set in place
and proceeded with their forked heron feather ornaments and the
red cord with which they bound their hair; and their turquoise ear
plugs and sea shell lip pendants."

(Florentine Codex VIII, ch. 14; fig. 69)

Woman's Song

http://www.nyupress.org/sisterstories/cuicacalli/womans.song.html

I did not know
what sort of creature
I was;
as time went on
I gradually became aware.

Then each day,
day after day,
I remained staring
after the many needle paths,
after the countless needle paths,
and in the paths of my needle
there would take form
many swirling patterns,
countless swirling patterns.
The upper clothing racks
and the lower clothing racks
would bend down under the weight
of the beautiful robes
which I had embroidered.
There was a brilliant glittering
over the clothing racks
where hung the beautiful robes
which I had embroidered.

One day
a young man
came.

<u>I married him.</u>
and we lived on.

               – from Ainu, "Song of a Human Woman"

Other

http://www.nyupress.org/sisterstories/tecuilhuitontli/other.html

What it really means <u>to be the outsider</u> is not sharing the
memories and history, and to be known only by my connection to
one of them. To him.

    I too was a sister. An eldest sister in a different land. I angered
them by wanting to leave and I was sent away.

    That works out perfectly, you might say. But nothing ever does
really. Still. . . . I can recognize the patterns. . . .

another's house

http://www.nyupress.org/sisterstories/calpulli/youth/
anothers.house.html

Being cast out of the house was the ultimate sanction with which
Mexica elders threatened the young:

    "Already in another's compound, <u>already in the entrance of
another's house</u>: With this saying were taught, were admonished
one's sons or the common folk, in order that no one might do an
improper, a bad thing; in order not to be driven forth, in order not
to be forced to wander to others' compounds, to others' house
entrances. He was advised:"

    "If you do something evil, you will be driven forth, you will be
made to wander in others' compounds, in the entrances of others'
houses."

                         (*Florentine Codex* VI, ch. 43)

the maize bin

http://www.nyupress.org/sisterstories/calpulli/maize.bin.html

A riddle:

    "What is that which is an old woman with hair of straw standing
at the house entrance?"

                "The maize bin." (*Florentine Codex* VI, ch. 42)

children

http://www.nyupress.org/sisterstories/calpulli/death/
death.children.html

A Mexica lord speaking to his son told him:
"The children who die become as precious green stones, as
precious turquoises, as precious bracelets. When they die they go
not where it is fearful, the place of sharp winds, the region of the
dead. They go there to the home of Tonacatecuhtli; they live in the
garden of Tonacatecuhtli, suck the flowers of Tonacatecuhtli, live
by the tree of Tonacatecuhtli; by it they suck."
"It is not in vain, oh my son, that children, babies, are buried in
front of the maize bin, for this signifies that they go to a good
place, a fine place, because they are still as precious green stones,
still as precious bracelets; still pure, they become as precious
turquoises."

(Florentine Codex VI, ch. 21)

Song of Otontecuhtli
In Nonoalco, in Nonoalco, is flowery scent
in shielding pines it clothes itself
this will not fall

In Nonoalco, the eagle cactus fruit
in cacao flowers clothes itself
this will not fall

I am the Tepaneca man Cuecuexin
I am Quetzalcoatl, Cuecuexin

I am just the god of wind bearing the obsidian blades
I am just the god of wind bearing the obsidian blades
⟨. . .⟩

Florentine Codex II, Appendix

To the expectant woman
A young Mexica man's elders greeted the news of the expected
birth of a child, saying to the woman:
"O my beloved granddaughter, o precious person, o precious
bracelet, o precious green stone, o precious turquoise, o hair, o
fingernail: now truly the god, the ruler, the lord of the near, of the
close, has remembered you. Within you he wanted to place a life;
he wanted to provide you with a precious necklace; he wanted to
provide you with a precious feather."

"Perhaps you have sighed? Perhaps you have wept? Perhaps you have reached out your arms to him? Perhaps you have begged our lord, the night, the wind, in the night, at midnight? Perhaps you have kept vigil? <u>Perhaps you have been industrious in sweeping and in offering incense</u>?"

"Perhaps for this reason it was determined above us, in the land of the dead, in the beginning, that our lord wished to place life within you? Perhaps it is true that the lord, our prince, Quetzalcoatl, Precious Twin, Precious Serpent, Green Feathered Twin, Green Feathered Serpent, the creator, the author, has permitted it? And perhaps Ome Tecuhtli, Ome Cihuatl, Two Lord, Two Lady, stated it? Perhaps their instruction was that a child be born."

(Florentine Codex VI, ch. 25)

Coatlicue sweeps

The story goes that while Coatlicue was living at Coatepec, she was in the habit of sweeping the place, as an act of devotion. The Nahuatl storytellers said:

"And once, when Coatlicue was sweeping, feathers descended upon her, what was like a ball of feathers. Then Coatlicue snatched them up; she placed them at her waist. And when she had swept, then she would have taken the feathers which she had put at her waist. She found nothing. Thereupon by means of them Coatlicue conceived."

(Florentine Codex III, ch. 1)

Ochpaniztli

http://www.nyupress.org/sisterstories/ochpaniztli.html

In Ochpaniztli, the feast of sweeping, Teteo Innan, the Mother Goddess, Toci, the grandmother, was honored.

She led the women curers in mock battle. And accompanied by the guardians of Chicome coatl, the lady Seven Serpent, Teteo Innan went scattering corn meal in the marketplace.

At midnight she died. The Nahuatl nobles told Sahagún: "No one spoke at all, none talked, nor did anyone cough; it was if the earth lay dead." The priests severed her head. One, wearing her skin, ran through the streets accompanied by warriors holding brooms, to the foot of the Coatepec where she met her son, Cinteotl, the maize, the skin of her thigh. And Cinteotl wore frost, Itztlacoliuhqui, the Curved Obsidian Knife, as his headdress.

Together they returned to the temple of Toci. At dawn, Teteo Innan was covered with eagle down on her head and legs and dressed in her eagle blouse and skirt. With the women curers Toci went to find her son, Cinteotl, and sent him to enemy land. She returned to her own home at Atempan.

Then the warriors assembled and the Speaker, the Tlatoani, seated on an eagle skin, gave them their weapons and insignia. And the older Mexica women said:

"These are our beloved sons whom we see here. If in five days, in ten days, the sea, the conflagration are announced, that is war, will they perhaps return? Will they perhaps make their way back? Truly, they will be gone forever."

And Toci and the women curers went singing and dancing. And the young women who carried the seed corn came, with feathers pasted on their arms and legs, and sang the song of Chicome coatl. And they scattered corn of all colors on the people.

Then chalk and feathers were brought down from the temple of Huitzilopochtli. And the warriors ran to the feathers, and when they seized them, the feathers billowed up and fell down.

(Florentine Codex II, ch. 30)

a fragment

http://www.nyupress.org/sisterstories/coatepec/fragment.html

I wonder what to do. In my travels around this sun wheel I have found a place where my sister has left something, a small thing, a chip from a jewel, a pin feather. A single space where she represents the ritual site, Hue Cuauhxicalli, the place of the Great Eagle Bowl, one of the sacred precincts of Tenochtitlan, the center of the world, the place where sun god and moon goddess died in the human images. She hasn't linked it.

She has not linked it and I wonder if she meant to leave it unlinked, that is, simply to set it off, a sacred place like the weathered wooden one-room hut of the Old Catholic Western-Rite Orthodox Parish of the Holy Transfiguration of Christ-on-the-Mount along Mead Mountain Road in Woodstock, neighboring the zen retreat, with its gold deer, young buddhas, sweet bells and bright painted, geometrically patterned windowframes, and near the trailhead below Overlook Point and the abandoned inn where Ulysses Grant once stayed a hundred years ago and where just months ago my son and I spent two exhausted hours trudging up the constant incline and found death smiling in the cliff winds and the swirling mist and then before coming down ate apples and gulped the too-small bottles of water we had brought, fighting the whole way down against our cramping, weary muscles and against the urge of gravity and our legs to walk off into the vector which bisects the downward slope and sky.

We did the same that day in autumn as we had the earlier time last Spring when Carolyn and I discovered the church, a day when I was crushed by hurt and loss and assailed by fears of madness and suicidal longings. Stopping briefly first in Red Hook for bread and coffee, and then following only an instinct to poke into the budding mountains, we came upon this mountain church, its wooden communion rail worn smooth, the gold thread of the altar cloth frayed and dim with years of light, and the painted tabernacle fading, the peace within less miraculous than a comfort when one was needed.

We did the same as then this Fall again after Jeremiah and I stumbled down the mountain on rubber legs. Just as in Springtime we drove back in to Woodstock and to the Gypsy Wolf Cantina, for chiles rellenos and Tecate, grilled fish with lime and cucumber sauce, in one season a wedding supper after a silent wedding, in another the feast following a rite of passage.

She has not linked it and I wonder if she's just forgotten. I search the wheel for the places which talk of the Speaker, the Tlatoani, and I link them here now, hoping only that in what I do that I act for her, just as yesterday I removed a stitch, a link, to write something there between the parts of that she had written and already stitched, replacing her stitches carefully with my own, not wishing to break what she had done into pieces.

reciprocity

http://www.nyupress.org/sisterstories/coatepec/reciprocity.html

If we wish to know the text our reader has written through her choices, we will have to reciprocate. She can only know by our choices what distinguishes her own. We construct the electronic text by our choices, but we only come to know what we have written by understanding the choices of others. . . . We understand from the third person what we have written in the first person, but only in the process of reading the second person.
                                          – Michael Joyce, "A Feel For Prose"

presence

http://www.nyupress.org/sisterstories/coatepec/presence.html

We are interested in a text as a place of encounter where we continually create the future. Yet we desire our future as we experience it to remain the mystery it is as we anticipate it. Our encounter with the future text thus carries with it what might be called the melancholy of history. The awkward light of dawn isolates into angles and instances a half-illuminated world of the shapes we desire to project upon its shadows.

> – Michael Joyce, "A Feel For Prose"

[the reading returns to **a fragment**, above, and from "Holy Transfiguration of Christ-on-the-Mount along Mead Mountain Road in Woodstock, neighboring the zen retreat, with its gold deer" links to]

The new voice of the
• Unity in print »»»

http://www.nyupress.org/sisterstories/brother/newvoice.html

Writing in the classical and Western traditions is supposed to have a voice and therefore to speak to its reader. A **printed book** generally speaks with a single voice and assumes a consistent character, a persona, before its audience.

> (from Jay Bolter, *Writing Space*)

The printed book
The printed book in today's economy of writing must do more: it must speak to an economically viable or culturally important group of readers. Printing has helped to define and empower new groups of readers, particularly in the nineteenth and twentieth centuries: for example, the middle-class audience for the nineteenth-century British novel. But this achievement is also a limitation. An author must either write for one of the existing groups or seek to forge a new one, and the task of forging a new readership requires great talent and good luck. »»»

> (from Jay Bolter, *Writing Space*)

And even a new
And even a new readership, brought together by shared interests in the author's message, must be addressed with consistency. No publisher would accept a book that combined two vastly different subject matters: say, European history and the marine biology of the Pacific, or Eskimo folklore and the principles of actuarial science. It would be hard to publish a book that was part fiction and part non-fiction. The material in a book must be homogeneous by the standard of some book-buying audience. »»»

> (from Jay Bolter, *Writing Space*)

The new voice of the
• Unity in print »»»

Writing in the classical and Western traditions is supposed to have
a voice and therefore to speak to its reader. A **printed book**
generally speaks with a single voice and assumes a consistent
character, a persona, before its audience.

(from Jay Bolter, *Writing Space*)

This strict requirement
This strict requirement of unity and homogeneity is relatively
recent. In the Middle Ages, unrelated texts were often bound
together, and texts were often added in the available space in a
volume years or decades later. Even in the early centuries of
printing, it was not unusual to put unrelated works between two
covers. However, it is natural to think of any book, written or
printed, as a verbal unit. For the book *is* a physical unit; its pages
are sewn or glued together and then bound into a portable whole.
Should not all the words inside proceed from one unifying idea
and stand in the same rhetorical relationship to the reader?

(from Jay Bolter, *Writing Space*)

Reading Sister Stories

In *Sister Stories* a joint declaration of our intent makes explicit our
goals. This simple action in fact reflects the common understanding
we have that our work *is* an act of communication, addressed to an
other whose evaluation we expect and indeed invite. This is only one
of several ways that we make our positions with respect to the interpretation of the past explicit in the text. Another, signed, text specifically identifies my intentions as an archaeologist. "Signing, then, is
the first step toward the truth of any situation. Only what is personalized can become available for clarification, wholeness, and interaction. Thus, the most important thing about any act is: did I do it and
do I accept responsibility for it, or do I behave as if someone else, or
nobody in particular, did it?" (Morson and Emerson 1990: 69–70,
commenting on Bakhtin 1993).

Through the development of *Sister Stories* I recognized that my
authoritative position entails a *responsibility* that needed to be made
explicit (compare Wolf 1992: 11). Archaeologists *are* invested with
authority and what we say about other cultures is seen as particularly

believable. We may be less entitled to speculation than nonarchaeologists, because our speculations rest on a relationship of trust with our publics (Lavine 1991; compare A. Praetzellis 1998: 1). I try to situate my authority as a product of strategies of active knowledge construction rather than as a side effect of the ownership of knowledge products. By including a statement of my own goals I acknowledge my own utopian desire to imagine pasts that are not affirmations of inevitable categorical devaluation of any human group. As I note, for the Mexica in particular this requires me to come to terms with the violence that others see as related to systematic degradation of women (e.g., Klein 1993, 1994, Nash 1978). Acknowledging this view, which I and others contest (e.g., Brumfiel 1996, Gillespie 1989, McCafferty 1988, 1991) is, for me, the only responsible strategy in creating the kind of seductively persuasive view of the past that is possible with new media.

At the same time, *Sister Stories* acknowledges multiple ways of knowing, and hence multiple sources of authority in interpretation. In an unsigned,[11] personalized fragment one of the contemporary writers reflects on becoming part of a family, as both a process of physical incorporation and of constructing shared memories. Constance Perin (1992: 207–11) found that, in museum exhibits – which I argue below are a nonelectronic form of hypertext presentation – "resonance with familiar subjects heightens interest" and allowed visitors to reach satisfactory judgments about the authenticity of presentations about other cultures. Visitors personalized and identified with exhibits, and were interested in stories of "material and cultural minutiae." Personalization of knowing is a common strategy not only for nonspecialists but for specialists, but one specialists seldom seem to acknowledge. The well-founded regard archaeology gives, as a discipline, to those among us who master traditional crafts in order to speak more knowledgeably about long-vanished technologies is perhaps the only legitimate voice in mainstream archaeology for this strategy. But is there a fundamental difference between our colleagues who can reproduce ancient forms of stone tools, and the writer in this fragment of *Sister Stories*, who knows in her own body what it is like to be confronted with a web of kin without any of the memories that draw them together?

At several points, *Sister Stories* exemplifies the multiple strategies for forging association that archaeological materials allow. As specialists we habitually search in map fashion through materials whose relations are those of juxtaposition, whether these are original research databases or texts in which these are reproduced. We examine visual representations for what we recognize as similarities. Yet we often find the same practices problematic when carried out by nonspecialists. Our anxiety to enforce the right linear pattern of thought is constantly undermined by the nonlinear nature of our own knowing. Until we engage in more direct exemplification of nonlinear analysis, and develop better critiques of just what makes some examples of these practices more satisfying, we will continue to fail in attempts to exercise our authority to police others who engage in associational strategies. We should recognize that the nonspecialists with whom we are in dialogue do not necessarily observe the boundaries we see between different domains of knowledge. Perin (1992: 207–11) found that museum visitors juxtaposed the knowledge they constructed at different exhibitions (even different museums), whether or not it could be easily accommodated in a single framework.

Making associations, it has been argued, binds together general human knowledge production, specialist knowing, writing, and hypertext as a medium (M. Joyce 1995: 22, 44–7). We may choose to call it ethnographic analogy, but associational memory is perhaps the most common strategy archaeologists use to create meaningful accounts of the past. The nonspecialist writers of *Sister Stories* exemplified associational understanding in many places in the work. A series of links proceed through connections between the basic narrative of work contained within the places in the space *Calpulli*, and the sentiments expressed in an Ainu song. Other texts included in *Sister Stories* portray the idealized life of young Aztec women as one of ceaseless work, epitomized by skilled textile production. This "work" recalls the pleasure the Ainu woman expressed in the cloth she made. Critical to the balancing act that a Bakhtinian perspective demands is recognizing likeness and difference at the same time.

As Carolyn Guyer (1996) writes:

We understand, or make meaning, largely by contrast and comparison, that is, what is different and what is like. Things that are alike seem to fall "naturally" into neighborhoods, classes, drawers, teams, and other categories. That seems easy enough. Or at least it is what we often do without thinking. In some ways, you could say this is a means of tending to history, or what is known. Contrasting what is different – or unknown – with what we already know catalyzes the process of making meaning. Known is the past, Unknown the future, memory and desire, these are always the components of the present. Without differences, therefore, we are not even alive, not even present.

The procedures we use as specialists to create analogies are not fundamentally different than those used by nonspecialists, and as the debates about analogy and the direct historic approach make clear, are no less contentious. But we have generally ruled out from the beginning certain sources of analogy, particularly those related to emotion, values, and personal experience. For many of the present-day others who engage in dialogues about the meaning of the past, it is only because of emotions, values, and personal experience that any of this matters (Layton 1989a, Lowenthal 1990, Schmidt and Patterson 1995, Tchen 1992). These concerns should be of significance to archaeologists as well, unless we want to pass by key features of past experience, to our disadvantage (Deetz 1998b: 95, Kus 1992).

At other points in *Sister Stories*, links allow associations between fragments of information from different categories, not unlike the specialist strategy of using multiple lines of evidence to produce stronger archaeological knowledge. A Mexica text that provides moral reinforcement for correct behavior through the threat of homelessness recalls links in the work that reiterate the symbolic importance of the house entrance: a riddle that describes the house entrance as the place where honored old women and maize bins are properly located; a description of the maize bin as the location where babies are buried; and a metaphoric equivalence between children and jewelry. Analogical associations and the use of multiple lines of evidence underwrite links between the words of midwives during preparations for childbirth, calendrical ceremonies in which relations of good women to their houses and children are invoked, and a modern text in which the writer is inspired to consider the possibility that a place in the mapped space is sacred in a way he understands by comparison with an equally foreign sacred place. In the contemporary text, the writer recounts the repeated lived experience of this contemporary sacred place, an example of the reflexive monitoring of daily practice that is central to Anthony Giddens's (1984) structuration theory. Does admitting that the source of this comparison, of the contemporary self-monitoring of structuration theory to ancient Mexica intertextuality, is a personal reflection, instead of the application of a model to material objectified as evidence, weaken the insight?

Reflexive monitoring of lived experience for meaningful measures of what experience might have been in the past is how *Sister Stories* operates for both its initial writers and later readers. The dialogic interplay of understanding the interpretive choices of others (from *fragment* to *reciprocity*) takes place through a process of constructing a story that makes sense of the juxtapositions made by others. "Not only do the choices a reader makes in an electronic text govern what she next sees, but they also unfold patterns for her discovery of the narrative *in much the same way that conversational cues shape our discovery of one another*" (M. Joyce, "A Feel for Prose,"; in M. Joyce 1995: 227–45; emphasis added). In standard archaeological discourse we offer phrases like "The figurine cache suggests . . . ," when in fact no set of objects speaks except through a voice we provide. Our revoicing of the material utterance of past authors is in turn addressed as a comment seeking the evaluation of those whom we address.

The link from *reciprocity* to *presence* comments on the openness of text, as a place where readers "create the future." Returning to *a fragment*, an attempt to follow the background of the modern sacred place, leads to a meditation on *The new voice of the* [book]. The loop through selections from J. David Bolter's *Writing Space* (1991) presents the dilemma for creating open-ended texts in traditional media. The western tradition of the book calls for a unity of voice; the modern economy of books calls for a voice to address a consuming market segment; and the expectation of the modern economy of books is that subject matter will be inherently related, not, for example, juxtaposing autonomous material from an ancient society with contemporary discussions of the associations nonspecialists make with that material, and reflexive commentary by specialists on the goals they have in presenting the autonomous material in the first place. *Sister Stories* is, in other words, impossible as a book.

Responsibility, Authority, and Multivocality

In my view, more effective archaeological presentations would capture more of the actual dialogic activity that characterizes the process of creating archaeological knowledge. *Sister Stories* attempts to do this by incorporating multiple voices engaged in actively attempting to understand one ancient society, that of early-sixteenth-century Tenochtitlan. The positionality of these voices is crucial to the effectiveness of the work; rather than achieving some kind of consensus, *Sister Stories* is shaped by multiple intentions, foregrounded as much as possible so that readers, in their creation of unique meaning, cannot fail to notice that what *they* are doing is exactly what Sahagún, my collaborators, and I have already done, each for our own reasons and from our own position.

Sahagún assembled texts in Nahuatl, provided by informants who most likely were elite males, and glossed them in Spanish. It is believed that he made use of a questionnaire or other formulaic device for eliciting information, thus of course channeling the responses of the Nahuatl-speaking informants (Lopez Austin 1974). It is known from surviving versions of his work that he assembled these already structured responses in successive orders. In the final version, Sahagún compiled and organized the texts he collected in multiple volumes under headings such as *Gods and Rites*, *The Calendar*, *Rhetoric*, *The Merchants*, *The Nobles*, and *The People*. In all, excerpts from 10 of the 12 "books" of the *Florentine Codex* were included in *Sister Stories*. The translators and editors of the *Florentine Codex* included some texts from other Sahagún manuscripts in appendices, and some of these are also included in *Sister Stories*.

Sahagún wrote from the perspective of a first-generation Spanish cleric seeking to understand Aztec society well enough to advance the process of conversion to Christianity. His texts began as an attempt to support translation efforts by enriching dictionary sources. The common characterization of Sahagún as an early ethnographer paradoxically stands in the way of evaluating his contribution, since it homogenizes his distinctive efforts as part of an anachronistic ethnographic task. In twentieth-century use, the term "ethnography" presumes a particular super-addressee and calls for a kind of evaluative response that would have been utterly irrelevant to the sixteenth-century author. In her critical examination of the use by archaeologists of sixteenth-century European narratives concerning native societies of the southeastern United States, Galloway (1992: 193) makes a related argument: if we take the narrative structure of such texts seriously, in order to use them as sources we must

> remove the interpretative apparatus constituted by all modifiers that express the narrator's and/or implied author's judgement of object, person, or action. . . . when such a process is carried out *in extenso* for one of these texts, an amazing thing happens: the story of Indian actions in response to invasion emerges from these tales of Spanish heroism like the transposition of figure and ground in a visual perception experiment. The resulting story of what the Indians did is still not comprehensible, *nor should it be*: we do not see all of it and it does not match our own or the Spaniards' master-scripts. But at last this version of events can be clearly seen to be incomprehensible in our terms, and we are no longer deluded by plausibility. (emphasis added)

As an author, Sahagún was not guided by the desire to convey a sense of the otherness of the Aztecs that would move his readers to new knowledge about themselves and about other cultures; he was engaged in an attempt to explain Aztec society in such a way and to the limited extent necessary to enable the work of conversion. For example, he reproduced the texts used by all modern researchers as evidence of life-cycle rituals (R. Joyce 2000a) only as models of persuasive Nahuatl rhetoric (compare Mignolo 1995: 208–9). He was not situated well to either receive or transmit an "ethnographic" assessment of gender relations in Tenochtitlan (Burshatin 1996; compare Arvey 1988, Brown 1983). But because he did not create his accounts monologically, but dialogically, through a process of communication with Aztec elders, the texts contain Bakhtinian echoes of "double-voiced" words that can be revoiced as echoes of the original Aztec speakers. As a result, while Sahagún's texts were not ethnographic in any meaningful sense, they do support reading from different perspectives. "What's found is not buried there as code but rather shines through: not Hansel's strewn breadcrumbs but rather Gretel's persistence of vision against the coming night" (M. Joyce 2000).

Thus, my goal was to resurrect echoes of other voices from Sahagún's texts. For me, *Sister Stories* is an attempt at an overtly feminist work about understanding Aztec women, understanding academic construction of knowledge about Aztec women, and understanding nonacademic construction of knowledge about Aztec women (compare Wolf 1992: 50–60, 118–23). My nonspecialist collaborators in the project share a concern with exploring gender difference from a realist perspective, but each of them necessarily occupies a unique position.

Michael Joyce (2000) writes that *Sister Stories* "explores ways to be women and men. Building from the mythological story of Coyolxauhqui sister to Huitzilopochtli, the text itself explores the nature of telling and of reading, of being inside and outside a story, a place, a field, a history, a text. That is, how things mean or/as the body: one story: multiple." Distinguishing his goals in hypertext writing from postmodernism as it has come to be understood, he explicitly frames the work we accomplished in *Sister Stories* as related to "Donna Haraway's situated knowledge ('*simultaneously* an account of radical historical contingency for all knowledge claims and knowing subjects ... *and* a no-nonsense commitment to faithful accounts of a 'real' world')" (Haraway 1991).

I connect this to other arguments by feminist philosophers, including Sandra Harding's (1991: 156, 161, 163) call for "strong objectivity":

> a strong notion of objectivity requires a commitment to acknowledge the historical character of every belief or set of beliefs – a commitment

to cultural, sociological, historical relativism. But it also requires that judgmental or epistemological relativism be rejected. . . . The notion of "strong objectivity" conceptualizes the value of putting the subject or agent of knowledge in the same critical, causal place as the object of his or her inquiry. . . . A notion of strong reflexivity would require that *the objects of inquiry be conceptualized as gazing back in all their cultural particularity and that the researcher, through theory and methods, stand behind them, gazing back at his own socially situated research project in all its cultural particularity.* (emphasis added; see Rose 1993, Wylie 1992a, Wolf 1992: 125–6)

Our goals, in other words, were not to create an anything-goes environment, but instead, to foreground the way that people in particular situations come to understand other cultures. As Carolyn Guyer and Martha Petry (1991) wrote in their introduction to an early collaborative hypertext,

deconstruction of priority is what we had in mind. We perceived the nature of connection as exactly the context of human relations, an impossible thing to say except through art, images, examples, stories from the continuum of stories. . . . The multiple dimension of connection is for us still an unfathomable mystery. Influence, conversation, disposition, drift. Some paradoxical concurrence by which individual voice becomes.

Sister Stories is several things at once, each of those things resulting from the operation of an individual author who is not erased, but rather exists in tension with all the other authors involved. The multivocal nature of constructions of the past is, I would argue, the central problem that archaeologists face in more accurately presenting the narratives through which we create knowledge. Creating multivocal hypertexts can be a way to both acknowledge the permeability of the boundaries between those with legitimate interests in talking about the past, and a way to try to explain and defend the specific responsibility we as archaeologists have incurred to past others through our engagement with their material remains.

Multivocal electronic narratives should not seek to resolve contending views. Instead, they have the potential to expose the ways people with different views differentially use material remains. The messiness introduced should be seen as a strength, and a microscale representation of the macroscale of healthy archaeological dialogue already extending between different texts. The ambiguities and contestation preserved in *Sister Stories* are, I would suggest, evidence of a *better* representation of the past according to the criterion of empirical adequacy which philosopher Alison Wylie (1992a, 1995), following Helen Longino, proposes archaeologists adopt in place of more reductive criteria. It would be difficult to create a single linear text that accomplished this. While the dangers of the medium – particularly anonymity of voices and the flattening of all information to the same degree of authority – cannot be evaded, they are actually not unique to electronic media (compare Wolf 1992: 54).

Telling Stories in Archaeology

Guyer and Petry's (1991) suggestion that human relations are best exemplified through stories echoes Bakhtin's repeatedly expressed view that novels present the best image of reality. The concreteness of images, examples, and stories has appealed to archaeologists of all theoretical orientations. Many of the dialogues discussed in chapter 3 were conceived of as forms for telling stories, not just as rhetorical devices for introducing multivocality. Standing in counterpoint to the we of the archaeological article, and more self-conscious I and you of dialogic texts, is the domain of the archaeological story, in which a speaking voice narrates in the third person. Story foregrounds the key difference in approaching narrative as voice rather than plot.

Deetz (1998b: 94) claims that telling stories is inescapable in archaeology: "What is it that we do, and why do we do it? Simply put, archaeologists *are* storytellers. It is our responsibility to communicate to as wide an audience as possible the results and significance of our findings." He explicitly approaches narrative as a way of addressing a specific audience, a wider public, in distinction to the narrow audience which will recognize and approve of the conventions of the standard research article. The voice selected in these different forms of archaeological narrative is directed at the other to whom the narrative is addressed; it is the form that the "sideways glance" takes in archaeological writing. In choosing to write "stories" archaeologists often take a position on the subject of the gap between the actual excitement that doing archaeology produces, and what is conveyed in conventional text (Spector 1993: 1–4; compare Boivin 1997, Stevens 1997). For many archaeologists who embark on this route, the imagined super-addressee is someone who is not a professional, someone perhaps that they might once have been. Yet many of these works actually find an audience primarily within the profession. This suggests that it is not only the desire to widen the audience that motivates archaeologists who write stories, but, as Adrian Praetzellis (1998: 1) intuits, the sense that some of the insights an archaeologist has come in the form of stories and cannot be easily reduced to conventional scientific writing.

In self-consciously attempting to tell stories, archaeologists enter into the terrain of writers of fiction, and take on the responsibility for the craft work involved. Like writers of fiction, archaeologists who succeed in constructing compelling stories that seem potentially real draw on small details. Their selection of details allows them to show, rather than tell (following Gass 1970: 55–76): to let an object condense meaning, to have a detail direct us to a thought, without leading us step by step through an argument for the association. As Lu Ann De Cunzo (1998: 42–3) wrote,

> telling these stories is far from easy. . . . The key to good stories, as to good scholarship, is details – an object, an action, a thought, a look. The stories I tell and the images I present here negotiate a difficult path. My imagination should paint in few of the details while allowing the stories to communicate the messages and meanings I intend.

Daniel Mouer (1998: 9) comments on how he found it necessary to think about the "language, costume, gesture" and other aspects of daily life in order to make the character in his historical archaeological story real: "It made the detailed groundedness of archaeological insight seem, somehow, all the more important."

Many archaeologists producing written narratives comment on the difficulty of capturing the sense of spoken language. As Robin Ryder (1998: 40) put it: "I have tried, as I wrote this story, to remember the cadence, rhythm, and word usages favored by the various informants I have encountered over the years." As William Gass (1970: 32) wrote of the challenge of producing believable fiction:

> a dedicated storyteller . . . will serve history best, and guarantee its popularity, not by imitating nature . . . but by following as closely as he can our simplest, most direct and unaffected forms of daily talk, for we report real things, things which intrigue and worry us, and such resembling gossip in a book allows us to believe in figures and events we cannot see, shall never touch.

Mouer (1998: 12–13) chose to present his story of seventeenth-century Virginia in the form of a petition, noting while that he lacked access to examples of spoken language he had petitions whose language he could emulate. Where he could not imagine the spoken word convincingly, he could use typography to give a sense of difference in time and place.

The challenges of speaking for a subject from another time and place are formidable. We risk reducing the others to whom we would like to give voice to "pretender doubles," monologic extensions of ourselves (Bakhtin 1990: 27–36, 59–61). The task required is to preserve a sense of the autonomy of the represented:

> The question arises as to whether science can deal with such absolutely unrepeatable individualities as utterances, or whether they extend beyond the bounds of generalizing scientific cognition. And the answer is, of course, it *can*. In the first place, every science begins with unrepeatable single phenomena, and science continues to be linked with them throughout. In the second place, science . . . can and should study the specific form and function of this individuality. . . . The text is the primary given (reality) and the point of departure for any discipline in the human sciences. . . . The real object is the social (public) [person], who speaks and expresses himself through other means . . . it is impossible to understand the deed [of the subject] outside its potential (*that is, re-created by us*) signifying expression . . . *it is as though we are causing [the subject] to speak* (we construct his important testimonies, explanations, confessions, admission, and we complete the development of possible or actual inner speech). (Bakhtin 1986: 108, 113–14; emphasis added)

For many archaeologists, this autonomy is something that is best guaranteed by the availability of the words of original speakers. In the most self-conscious of the stories constructed from the words of past speakers, the archaeologist-author maintains a clear awareness of their reaccentuation of the original word. Rebecca Yamin (1998: 74) exploits the possibilities of juxtaposition to create a narrative in which literary references depicting the Five Points neighborhood in New York City as a slum are countered by "homely stories that may be told from the recent archaeological and historical research conducted on one block." Yamin describes her purpose as "to thicken the plot." She notes that

> constructing narratives, albeit through the lens of my politics and my present, gave us a sense of the neighborhood that we did not have before and led to a depth of understanding that is different than anything I have ever reached with archaeological data. The telling of a story is more than a style of presentation; *it becomes a way of knowing*. By having to order facts in a plot . . . the historian comes to understand. (Yamin 1998: 84)

Meskell (2000) draws on original Egyptian texts to frame her narrative of the human life cycle, juxtaposing these with descriptions of material remains that are not directly part of the textual record. By occupying the position of interlocutor with both the texts and the material remains, she opens up the narrative possibilities of her example beyond the concerns of past subjects while simultaneously maintaining grounding in the lives of those subjects.

Two of the most widely cited archaeological stories, among the most influential texts of feminist archaeology, were written by Janet Spector (1991) and Ruth Tringham (1991) as contributions to a volume stemming from a conference. As a result, they arguably share a common language and at least partly, are addressed to the same audience. At the same time, they present very different positions with respect to the availability of resources for visualizing past subjects. Spector (1991, 1993) writes about a known, named person who can be placed in the archaeological site she explored, the nineteenth-century Wahpeton Dakota village Inyan Ceyaka Atonwan, through the use of written texts. Tringham writes about a known, unnameable person, who can be placed in the site of Opovo through the material traces of actions in the past. Tringham's original narrative occupies less than a page, and imagines the participation of one member of the Opovo society in the deliberate burning of a house, vividly imagining her reactions in a first-person internal dialogue. Spector produced a five-page narrative that covers events over the space of a few months.

Tringham's story is tightly tied to the specific evidence of the intense burning of one house, so that her protagonist in a sense reproduces the archaeological focus on this material. But in the course of the brief narrative, she supplies evocative hints at the disadvantaged position of the imagined narrator, a younger woman married into the household from a larger village, to which she wants to return. The narrative proposes an entire system of social relations, a gendered order that underlies much of the archaeology of early farming societies. By personifying the social position of the powerless younger woman, Tringham gives a voice to someone who otherwise has none, to one of the little-regarded people of history who tend to fall out of archaeological accounts. Her experiment in writing this narrative, and the cycle of additional stories she has created as part of her ongoing work, the Chimera web (Tringham 1998, 2000: 124–6), draws strong reactions, contesting her choice of vantage points, her assignment of names, images, and personalities to the people she is imagining, but little objection to either her explication of the house burning or the model of gender relations she is exploring. It seems risky to many who see and hear the work to imagine real people, even when this act of imagination comes embedded in a dense, truly multivocalic hypertext with layers of auto-critique.

In contrast, the reaction to Spector's imagination of the circumstances surrounding the loss of a bone-hafted awl, which connects it to Mazaokiyewin, the historically attested daughter of Mazomani and Hazawin, has generally been positive, despite the fact that Spector supplies these actual people with motivations and thoughts to which she of course has no access. This raises interesting questions about the way that archaeologists think about the characters they narrate. On the surface, it should be more problematic to impute motivations, feelings, and thoughts to someone who actually lived, and who cannot speak for themselves. Tringham's practice of making up plausible personifications of the types of persons who are implicit in theoretical perspectives can do no violence to the actual thoughts and motivations of someone who was never more than a fictional character.

One way to view the general comfort that archaeologists have had with fictionalizing real people, not only in "What this Awl Means" but in the other historical narratives discussed above, is to propose that none of the archaeologists writing these stories actually are trying to imagine the past. Instead, they are creating a link between the past and themselves in the present. Most dramatically, Spector (1991: 401) makes the loss of the bone awl a pivotal omen in her story:

> Both mother and daughter knew that the awl handle was an object of the past, not of the future. But when the handle was lost, it saddened them more deeply than they could explain. One evening as they stored the last of the harvested corn they laughed together remembering the "prayer-man" Riggs and his ideas about men planting corn. Then for some reason each thought of the antler awl handle and they shared their sadness about its loss. They realized that the feeling of loss they experienced wasn't simply about the small tool. Instead, they discovered each shared a pervasive sense of loss about the past and, even more, they felt troubling premonitions about the future.

While both stories are presented as views of events in the past, Spector's narrative comments on events after the fact. Johannes Fabian (1991: 192) writes that

> omens do not become omens by being perceived. . . . Omens become omens only by being told. . . . Events acquire meaning as omens when we construct them as a past for narratives to build on. That we construct that past in the form of a future . . . is, in my view, no objection

to the thesis that *in ominous experiences contemporaneous events are being related to the person who experiences them as essentially past. . . .* So, an event that is present . . . is construed as past.

The central action in "What this Awl Means" has the effect of actually bringing the future, from which Spector is writing, into the past, as the unarticulated but inevitable outcome of events. As she writes in her rich explication of the resources she used to create the narrative, and of her own motivation for writing in this new way, she is interested in conveying her own empathetic sense of connection to the material traces she recovered archaeologically. "In response to this evocative find, I wrote the story of how the awl might have been used and lost. In many ways, that work represents the culmination of what I have learned" (Spector 1993: 18). Spector's narrative is primarily an externalization of the work her imagination had to accomplish to think about material culture at the scale of a person, even though that is not one of the goals she explicitly cites for this ambitious work.

Spector (1993: 17) lists three very interesting goals for the monograph commenting on the narrative: she "wanted to incorporate Dakota voices, visions, and perspectives into the story"; she "wanted to highlight women's activities and the relations between men and women"; and she "wanted to communicate in an easily accessible way" what she had learned about the community. I have already noted that seeking a wider audience is not the sole, or even most significant, motivation for experimental writing in archaeology. But it is without a doubt one of the constant motivations expressed by archaeologists who invest the substantial time and energy in teasing out material implications that could be presented in traditional formats, and then go on to spend even more time and effort to create alternative representational media. The urge to make ideas about the past intelligible to others outside the discipline might be understood in terms of the literal remaking of the boundaries of archaeological interpretation that is a marked part of the contemporary experience of archaeology. Archaeologists, no longer in control of dialogues about past materiality (if we ever were), want to remain part of the conversation. New forms of writing are directed outward, seeking their response.

Recovering Voice in Archaeology

In fact, of course, archaeologists already engage in multivoiced knowledge construction, but our disciplinary practices have tended to erase or limit acknowledgement of the heteroglossia of our texts. The problems we think are important are set by the prior writings of others, which themselves were created in expectation of a response. In our own research, we both respond to others and launch our own calls for answers into the dialogue of archaeology. Archaeological activity takes place through an assembly of utterances and responses constrained by forms and formats, which begin their lives both signed and personalized and end as indirect cited speech, revoiced by the acknowledged authors of research reports. And even so, we have many conventions intended to mark the inherent polyphony of archaeological activity: the contributions of specialists as signed appendices; footnotes naming specialists, or even entire field crews; and of course, the intertextuality of citations. What we have not perhaps been able to do is achieve a level of comfort with unfinalizability, the open-endedness that our field process has traditionally been aimed to overcome.

Archaeological discourse strains to contain the determination of the past within specific disciplinary contexts: but the past always escapes us, as it should, since it is not our past (alone).

> We utter pronouncements like, "not very good writing/painting/thinking" in comparing works which supposedly partake of the same context, an anthology, a workshop, or a classroom. It may be perfectly valid to recognize that in the same anthology, for instance, some works will be better-written than others. But exactly what establishes a context isn't always easy to determine. The covers of a book, or the walls of a classroom, are not necessarily enough to keep their "contents" – human minds – perfectly contained. Boundaries are usually more permeable than we think. If we were to attempt to track how contexts continually reconfigure themselves, we would probably find it isn't possible to cross-index enough. . . . The concept of mastery is what propels the criticism "not very good" which, as criticism, is always a comment about a difference in skill or knowledge. Yet even mastery is a relative thing to the extent that it is based on a chosen idea of what makes some work preferable to others. (Guyer 1996)

Or as Bakhtin insists, no context is ever "the same."

In a very few cases, archaeologists have recognized (responded to) new insights from nonspecialists (compare Baker 1989). Tim Murray (1993: 114) cites the comments made by Bill Neijie, an indigenous Australian, on the public experience of a rock art site:

> Some *balanda* [white people] who come to Ubirr don't really understand what they see. They rush through the sites and then back to their

buses. They don't stay long enough at the sites. How can they understand? Some ways to make them understand better are:

    1. I would like more signs like the ones already at Ubirr to tell
the balanda what the painting is and the Aboriginal story about the
painting. . . .

    2. The stories about my country should be made bigger. . . . I would
like a big history book to be written where the stories could all be told.
This could be sold to visitors. I think the *balanda* story about the old
people [prehistory] could also be told.

Some of the most engaging contemporary archaeological writing,
works that exploit the possibilities of narrative and dialogue to the
fullest, have been produced in the more ephemeral media addressed
to nonspecialists: students, tourists, and visitors to sites. A series
of five interpretive booklets published by the University of New
England and the Yarrawarra Aboriginal Corporation reproduce
"stories from Aboriginal people, archaeology, oral history, maps, and
photographs" with the intention "to make visible some of the stories
of this landscape that have not been previously visible to non-
indigenous people" (Somerville, Beck, Brown, Murphy, Perkins, and
Smith 1999: 5). The booklets use different typefaces to represent distinct voices, which are also signed and dated. The voices of archaeologists and community elders are juxtaposed and create a cumulative
effect of multiple stories. Archaeological field notes serve as captions,
and document the poetic language that was captured at this first level
of on-site writing: "the midden was so obvious on the beach for so
many years, so dense it was almost shocking, so robust it was almost
edible – shell, bone, stone" (Somerville, Beck, Brown, Murphy,
Perkins, and Smith 1999: 24). The booklets also include brief site
reports in which narratives of intention and action rapidly and clearly
sketch out the field research and results, complete with bar graphs,
discussions of chronometric dates, and artifact identifications (Brown,
Beck, Murphy, Perkins, Smith, and Somerville 2000: 14–17, 32–3;
Murphy, Beck, Brown, Perkins, Smith, and Somerville 2000: 14–15,
24–9; Somerville, Beck, Brown, Murphy, Perkins, and Smith 1999:
28–31). Embedded in a narrative of place, the archaeological
reports work both as alternative forms of knowing the place, and as
clearly positioned voices with a unique, and consequently valuable,
perspective.

    The production of narratives with an eye toward the public pro-
vides an extraordinary opportunity to foreground the context that
distinguishes the archaeological voice, through dialogue with non-

archaeologists. Rebecca Yamin (1998: 83–4) reports on the creation of 22 "narrative vignettes" for the archaeological features documented on one block in New York City, as a means to "integrate the various lines of evidence in some way that would allow us to know, or at least speculate, on what it all meant." She notes that

> With the exception of the name, Phoebe, attributed to the mother of the newborn babies deposited in the privy associated with the brothel, nothing in the narratives is fictional, but everything cannot be taken as truth either. The stories are a kind of hermeneutic exercise in drawing the strands of information into a coherent whole. The construction of a narrative vignette provides a methodological beginning point. It forces the scholar to go out on a limb – to interpret what it all might mean – and *it allows any interested party, either professional or non-professional*, to question the interpretation and/or add to it. Most importantly, the process of writing a narrative tells you what you don't know thereby providing a reason to keep searching. (Yamin 1998: 85; emphasis added)

Adrian Praetzellis (2000) takes the impulse to tell a story for those outside the discipline, emergent in the irruption of dialogues in Matthew Johnson's (1999) and Ian Hodder's (1999) recent introductory texts, to its fullest expression. *Death by Theory* embeds its entire pedagogical intention in an entertaining story about an archaeologist – not coincidentally trying to write an innovative textbook – involved in an on-site mystery. The book plays with the popularity of mysteries with archaeological settings, but brings to the task an eye for the reality of field experience that recalls the more endearing aspects of Flannery's (1976) dialogues. Refreshingly direct statements of opinion by the authors are found in all three of these recent books, whose audience is clearly primarily students.

The Form of the Content

Like my colleague Ruth Tringham (1998), I believe that electronic media provide a unique environment for efforts to construct multiple narratives, one we must exploit to the fullest. But they are not a requirement for such narratives. As Michael Joyce (1995) writes, "All text is hypertext." Archaeology already exists in a disciplinary framework provided with multiple modes of knowledge presentation to which we might profitably return, and which we can use as a point of renewal. Museum exhibits are arguably nonelectronic, nonlinear dialogues between disciplinary specialists and the public. They provide some useful reflection on what is to be gained, and what challenges exist, in creating nonlinear, multivocalic texts.

Relationships between voice and authority have been a critical focus in recent museum practice (Lavine 1991; Smith 1994: 142–3). The realizations reached in the process should be entirely familiar by now:

> objects have no voice . . . the challenge . . . is to achieve a high degree of authenticity in [the curatorial] voice as measured against the best current scholarship. . . . The attendant demystification of objects may in fact bring them closer to the lives of visitors and release emotional and imaginative possibilities. All this requires a fine tact if the museum's interpretive authority is to be maintained. . . . [There is] a social contract between the audience and the museum, a socially agreed-upon reality that exists only as long as confidence in the voice of the exhibition holds . . . that contract must be maintained in the highly theatrical environment in which the event of the visit takes primacy over any object, label, or explanation and in which the visitor is inevitably a co-creator of any meaning. (Lavine 1991: 152–3)

Museum anthropologists have labored to break down the anonymous authority of museum exhibits, in favor of recognizing the local production of knowledge by multiple authors, through a number of now standard practices (Lavine 1992). Exhibits increasingly are created by teams, often featuring liaisons to communities whose cultural heritage is being incorporated. In larger museums, such teams routinely include staff charged with public education, who take as their task ensuring that the story told addresses a non-specialist audience. Exhibit teams may include multiple curators, especially when materials at issue are the cultural heritage of groups with recognized contemporary traditions descendant from those under discussion in the exhibit.

The exhibit planning process, consequently, may be seen as a multivocal, collaborative, dialogic form of knowledge production, ultimately responsible to the materiality of specific things with an existence separate from the exhibit team itself or its concerns (see Tchen 1992). In planning, members of the team will voice many threads of narrative, not necessarily all harmonious. Contradictions, partial knowledge, absence, are all implicit in the exhibit planning process.

The "final product" of exhibit planning is the ultimate in open narratives. It will consist of a spatial arrangement of things and different forms of comment on those things – texts of various sorts, drawings, photos, videos – loosely connected by an overarching narrative. Within that space, both literal and metaphoric, will hang fragments of many stories, representing many ways of thinking about specific things. Even when an exhibit team attempts to channel visitors through an exhibit according to a single preferred path (by employing docent tours, or using audio guides), they can never force visitors to engage with all the stories they offer, nor restrain visitors from creating their own novel narratives. All they can do is provide an example of close and respectful attention to the material base on which we construct our narratives.

Constance Perin's ethnographic research on museum exhibit design and reception documents that "the relationship between exhibitions and what audiences carry away is not linear, but rather it is complexly mediated by myriad factors, not least of which are audiences' repertoires of prior knowledge, semantic systems, and interpretive frames" (1992: 184). She suggests some of the constraints on the construction of narratives by museum visitors, constraints that may be equally applicable to other forms of archaeological narrative (Perin 1992: 207–11). Museum visitors displayed "resistance to assimilating the unfamiliar," something Perin characterized as "conservation": a desire to conserve what they already know by fitting new information alongside it. She found that "resonance" with already familiar subjects allowed visitors to reach satisfactory judgments about the authenticity of presentations about other cultures. Visitors personalized exhibits. But at the same time, visitors approached museums as institutions offering broader views: they *expected* alternative theories, they *expected* connections between the past, present and future – and they cross-related the knowledge they constructed at different exhibitions, even different museums.

Museum visitors understand their active role in the production of museum narratives and what Lavine (1991: 152) calls the "social contract" with museum authority. It is part of the reason visitors continue to seek out museums (and increasingly, on the World Wide Web, museum sites). Museum exhibits are a major genre in which nonspecialists actively experience themselves as authors providing the coherence to the stories being told. And part of what nonspecialist visitors want from scholars is, paradoxically, authoritative statements: not to close off their role as coauthors, but to incorporate along with their own experience of the material things, into their own storytelling.

We need to foreground the *activity* of knowledge production, and not knowledge *products* (compare Cruikshank 2000: 68–70). Guyer (1992) adopts Deleuze and Guattari's (1988) trope (already borrowed

from Pierre Boulez) of "smooth" and "striated" experience as a way
to think about

> Acceptance and Control, that is, occupying without counting, and
> counting in order to occupy. One is not preferable to the other; rather,
> neither exists without the other, which means that the only thing we
> can truly be interested in is the complex mixtures of the two, how they
> proportion themselves as they move through each other. . . . Closure,
> resolution, achievement, the objects of our lives are inventions that
> operate somewhat like navigational devices, placemarkers if you will.
> We go on like waves unsure of the shore, sometimes leaping backwards
> into the oncoming, but always moving in space–time, always finding
> someplace between the poles that we invent, shifting, transforming,
> making ourselves as we go. Hypertext as a literary re-forming em-
> bodies this unreasonably logical creative urge. . . . We are the *experi-
> ence* of learning. (emphasis added).

Archaeologists seem to be poised to see acknowledgement of multivocality as a threat to a real world. Contradiction is collapsed with
disorder, unnecessarily so.

Conventional archaeological texts operate with many of the same
forms of rhetoric as collaborative texts created with nonspecialists,
but do so within a distinct genre, the site report, which establishes an
imaginary boundary between professional archaeologists and their
public audiences. Stories and dialogues, the self-conscious narratives
of archaeology, routinely mark themselves out from the naturalized
narratives of conventional site reports and articles, to which they are
meant to be alternatives. Inadvertently, experimental writing stressing
their narrative difference can reinforce the authority of dominant
naturalized narratives. The difference that self-conscious archaeological narratives do need to attempt to maintain is that between the
narrator/author and the narrated subjects, including previous archaeologists cited in heteroglossic dialogue, collaborators in the work of
field, lab, and classroom, and archaeological publics.

The current ferment of new writing in archaeology points us
toward several possible ways to proceed. One way is to tell multiple
stories in multiple voices, as *Sister Stories* does. A second would be to
narrate in fragments, making the form of the reader's engagement
mimic the form of the archaeologist's engagement with the world, as
Jeanne Lopiparo (chapter 4) and Ruth Tringham (1998) both advocate.
And above all, we need to tell multiple stories about the same material, in multiple media and formats, from the conventional article to
the imaginative narrative.

6

The Return of the First Voice

With apologies to Clifford Geertz (1973, 19) what do archaeologists do? – they write

Ian Hodder (2000: 16)

With apologies to Ian Hodder, "What do archaeologists do? – They talk." We also dig, certainly. But we have always talked, and still talk, *as* we dig. The process of digging may be surrounded by paper, drawings, clipboards, pens and pencils, graph paper, tapes, masking tape, cameras, total stations, etc. – but it is also surrounded by voices. And while the paraphernalia of writing involves a "turning away" from excavation, the shaping of representation through narrative goes on at the *same* time as the bodily engagement of digging. By the time we come to inscribe our representations, they are already shot through with their prior voicing, which of course extends beyond the field into the classroom and the meeting room.

Telling Stories: The Forms of Archaeology

Narrativization is an activity through which analogical connections between different kinds of knowledge are given an aura of factuality, and thus naturalized, by the sequences of action through which they are joined. As Hayden White (1978: 134, 1987: 58–82) insists, narrative histories are exercises of power within specific social systems, and this is equally true of historical narratives produced by archaeologists. The status of archaeological narratives as exercises of power requires critical self-consciousness and puts into question the motivation and use made of archaeological knowledge (Shanks and Tilley 1987: 14, 25–7, 245–6). But Bakhtin (1984: 166) suggests that foreclosure of the dialogic construction of meaning can never really be successful (compare Shanks and Tilley 1987: 19–20). The perspective on narrative offered by Roland Barthes, briefly summarized in chapter 1, provides a way to examine why this should be so, and how in particular in archaeological writing narrative openness can be deliberately fostered.

Archaeological remains do not present themselves already embedded in a uniquely persuasive story. Instead, what archaeologists deal with in practice are ambiguous traces whose very description is problematic (Bradley 1997: 62–3, Hodder 1999: 66–9, Gero 1996). Drawing on scraps of meaning that they carry in memory, archaeologists place these traces into circulation as echoes of other stories. Beginning with a kind of still life, the archaeologist suggests a possible history for the material recognized as significant. The procedure is not unlike that Barthes (1977b: 73) described for the production of meaning from the "pregnant moment" in drawings, theater, and film: "in order to tell a story, the painter possesses only one moment ... [the image] will be a hieroglyph in which can be read at a glance ... the present, the past, and the future, i.e. the historical meaning of the represented gesture." The act of reading the "historical meaning" of the tableaux is by nature indeterminate, since many possible sequences of action could precede it (Barthes 1977d: 38–9). For the constructed images he examined, Barthes suggested that the social or shared nature of gestures and their conventionalized meanings supplied the grounds for choice between alternative interpretations (Barthes 1977b).

The interpretation of archaeological traces is also based on shared and social experience that grounds the production of meaning. The source of the pressure that leads to common recognition, and of the floating chains of signifieds that are reproduced, is the crystallization of archaeology as a field through the circulation of its narratives as dialogues. The signs united in archaeological narratives are bound in a relationship of "double implication: two terms presuppose one another," transforming chronological order to a logical binding "capable of integrating backwards and forwards movements" through the narrative (Barthes 1977c: 101, 120–2). What is represented as a sequence of action is transformed into a causal chain, where each step leads inevitably to what follows. Narrative "seems to found in nature the signs of culture" (Barthes 1977d: 45–6; see also 1977c: 116). The boundary-creation involved is what Michael Herzfeld (1992: 79) calls *disemia*, "a mode of organizing social knowledge through cultural form": "relations between insiders and outsiders ... always remain predicated on the distinction between the inside and the outside of whatever social group is in question."

Among the most important ways that archaeological narratives transform ambiguity into conventionalized meaning are the persuasive devices employed in archaeological texts. Following Bakhtin, rather than approach the existence of genres from a Formalist perspective in which unity is provided by the use of specific elements, I suggest that archaeological genres can more profitably be understood as drawing on specific chronotopes and engaging specific dialogues. Like the hybrid texts Barthes (1977d) examined, in which visual and linguistic materials served to "anchor" (channel) and "relay" (expand) interpretation, archaeological texts commonly take the form of mixtures of words and images. Graphics are thus yet another set of languages employed by archaeologists, and they communicate far more than the manifest content suggested by their captions (Molyneaux 1997, Moser 1992, 1998).

Moser (1998) has elegantly demonstrated that representations of human origins in archaeology employ a graphic language that comes to us inflected with meanings from centuries of European visual representation. The iconography she explores contributes to the heteroglossia of archaeology, introducing into its visual language the echoes of other places and times. As Moser (1998: 171) notes,

> by using familiar settings and projecting elements of our own existence back into the past, these images seem inherently reasonable as interpretations of that past. The fact that they satisfy a basic need for narrative and shared experience is critical to their success, reflecting how the primary function of the imagery is to reassure us of our relationship or connection to the distant past. . . . Archaeological imagery did not simply replace older images when new data were found, but rather incorporated new into the old pictures.

Contemporary archaeological works commonly present spatial maps that provide three-dimensional detail on the material contexts that were investigated, whether the medium is a contour map, a series of plans and profiles, or artifact section and plan drawings. These are not simply "'afterimages' of verbal ideas . . . provided to 'brighten up' the text . . . peripheral to the arguments being presented by authors" (Moser 1998: 15). Instead, Moser (1998: 16) identifies three features of scientific images that are relevant to archaeology: images actively constitute theories (they do not merely represent them); they may represent ideas not otherwise presented in text, including ideologies; and they are particularly persuasive, because they communicate in ways less consciously analyzed than those of text, using visual features to "fill in the gaps in a theory."

The circulation of images is a fundamental part of the dialogic reproduction of archaeology. Richard Bradley (1997) demonstrates that learning to draw in a particular style shapes the way that archaeologists see. He documents the propagation of "craft traditions" in archaeological visual representation as "individuals and groups acquire the ability to see hitherto unexpected phenomena . . . there follows a period of re-education in which other people learn to do the same, and, lastly, a phase of acceptance in which excavators come to terms with those observations and treat them as straightforward, even commonplace" (Bradley 1997: 66–8). The visual representations produced can be viewed as utterances addressed toward the others who evaluate, and in Bradley's account, ultimately accept (and reinscribe) them.

Archaeological texts strive to present sufficient visual representations to allow a reader educated in the conventions employed to imagine the original material in its three-dimensional form. "A single inscription would not inspire trust," as Bruno Latour (1999: 28) observes of the practices of scientists collaborating in a multidisciplinary ecological study. Part of the nature of archaeological persuasion is deeply lodged in a material rhetoric, in which things demonstrate the truth of assertions made about them. As Michael Shanks (1997: 74) has argued, archaeological photography is presented as a kind of documentary witness that can say "look and see for yourself," underwriting the "I was there" of the archaeologist. A kind of hyperrealism in graphics is a standard archaeological language that substitutes for an assumption of trust in the author.

But at the same time, archaeological texts employ a quite distinct graphical language which turns away from the project of three-dimensional simulation (James 1997: 22) to offer instead analytic representations that are mediated by measuring devices which promise objectivity.

We move now from the instrument to the diagram . . . paper, assimilable by every article in the world, and transportable to every text. The geometric form of the diagram renders it compatible with all the geometric transformations that have ever been recorded since *centers of calculation* have existed. What we lose in matter through successive reductions . . . we regain a hundredfold in the branching off to other forms that such reductions – written, calculated, and archival – make possible. (Latour 1999: 54–5)

Tables of measurements of artifacts, the use of standardized color charts, and graphical representations of these analytical observations are added to the text, even the most experimental (for example, Costello 1998: 71–3).

That representations of "objective" data are rhetorical is well established in the history of science. "The scientific text is different from all other forms of narrative. It speaks of a referent, *present* in the text, in a form other than prose: a chart, diagram, equation, map or sketch. Mobilizing its own *internal* referent, the scientific text carries within itself its own verification" (Latour 1999: 56; compare Lynch and Woolgar 1990, Baigrie 1996). The potential of visual displays of quantitative information to persuade viewers to misleading conclusions has been thoroughly explored (Tufte 1983, 1990). The choices made, even of font size and style, promote particular kinds of receptions.

As with textual representations in archaeology, it is no accident that the same kinds of graphics are reproduced over and over. The conventional forms of what Latour calls "diagrams" are one example of what he describes as "circulating references": "the many practices that end up in articulating propositions . . . the quality of the chain of transformation, the viability of its circulation," where "propositions" are "what an actor offers to other actors," with "actors" including both the humans and nonhumans that make up a science (1999: 309, 310). Graphics are dialogic as much as texts, connecting speakers (both human and nonhuman) in a chain of transformations through which archaeological meaning is communicated. Following in a line of existing graphical arguments is a dialogic engagement that seeks an affirmative evaluative judgment from others (compare Moser 1998: 17–18, Salazar 1993: 110–11). Innovation in a graphic display would risk negative evaluation or no response at all.

The rhetorical status of all visual and textual representations requires us to examine the archaeological genre which has functioned as the implicit background for the experimental writing discussed in the preceding chapters. This is the scientific article or site report. The format has been deeply naturalized. Jean-Claude Gardin (1992: 101) argued that interpretive and empiricist archaeological texts are "two natural kinds" that cannot be subjected to comparative evaluation, and then proceeded to propose that "the rules of the first genre are well known: they are those of the 'logico-scientific paradigm' . . . as for the rules of the second genre . . . narrative . . . we know precious little." Gardin (1992: 100–1) predicted that traditional forms of archaeological publications would be replaced by new symbolic forms, specifically data structures that would "provide more efficient and less costly forms of access to specialized knowledge" leading to "the end of printed documents and libraries."

Rather than following this logical evolutionary path, the scientific report remains alive and well, the dominant form of writing in archaeology. And far from being opposed to narrative, scientific articles are nothing but narratives: narratives that obscure the speaking voice, that presume a very select super-addressee, and that use "professional jargons, generic languages, languages of generations and age groups, tendentious languages, languages of the authorities, of various circles and of passing fashions, languages that serve the specific sociopolitical purposes of the day, even of the hour" (Bakhtin 1981: 262–3) to establish the chronotope of the archaeological discipline as a space–time of its own. Any example would do for the purposes of analysis. In the interest of reflexivity, I examine my own mortuary analysis of over 200 burials from the site of Tlatilco, Mexico (R. Joyce 1999b), an analysis which has the advantage for my purposes of having been presented multiple times in expanding dialogue and ultimately, in explicitly narrative form (R. Joyce in press a, in press b).

Science and the Erasure of the Speaking Voice

The starting point for my analysis was the publication of a catalogue of burials excavated over several years at Tlatilco, a village dating to ca. 1200–700 BC, located in the highlands of central Mexico (Garcia Moll, Juarez Cossio, Pijoan Aguade, M.E. Salas Cuesta, and M. Salas Cuesta 1991). The catalogue itself is an excellent example of the construction of specific forms of archaeological knowledge through exclusion of other forms. It included a listing of contents for each burial, a single map showing the location of the burials, and a variety of drawings of individual burials or sets of burials. Underlying the presentation of information was the adoption of two spatial scales as the only ones of relevance: the site as a whole, and the individual burial. My beginning assumption, in contrast, was that since mortuary rituals are designed and carried out by social groups, patterned remains could be examined as evidence of habitual practices that simultaneously created commonality and distinction between social groups. I consequently needed a way to represent a level between the individual and the whole site.

Previous statistical analyses had taken the entire set of burials as a single population and, through cluster analyses, arrived at specific observations about differences between female and male, adult and juvenile burials, and a set of practices that were interpreted as signs of social ranking across the site (Serra and Sugiura 1987, Tolstoy 1989). Iron-ore mirrors, necklaces, greenstone and shell objects, were found in a small group of burials interpreted as a top social rank composed of individuals of mixed age and sex (Tolstoy 1989: 109–12, Serra and Sugiura 1987). These observations, while undoubtedly accurate, were based on viewing each buried person as an individual independent of his or her social group. My own analysis treated burials clustered together as possibly resulting from the actions of a social group whose practices might have been relatively regular over time and distinct from those of other groups at each point in time.

My approach to demonstrating this point was to employ the tools of statistical analysis, coding each object in each burial as a variable and testing all relationships between categories for strength of association (R. Joyce 1999b: 22). The normal means of illustrating this procedure would have been to provide a series of tables, which in fact I did construct. But the cases in those tables were still the individual burials and the population of burials as a whole. The tables told, not the story I wanted to advance, but one which came to me already voiced from earlier authors. Not only the specific authors who had analyzed parts of this site before, but all contemporary practitioners of mortuary analysis were the other parties for whose utterances I was an addressee. As Bakhtin argues, I had the responsibility to answer these earlier voices with an evaluative judgment. By choosing to use some of their language – the statistical techniques and measures of strength – I affirmed my participation in the dialogue they advanced. But my choice to represent my results in a fundamentally different way revoiced the dialogue of mortuary analysis. Only by doing so could I possibly shift the focus toward the new kind of knowledge I wanted to create through my study.

Even here, however, I did not move outside the languages of archaeology for my response. Instead, I employed other already-voiced words, that would be both recognized by my addressees and seen as reaccented. I presented my results in the form of maps marking those burials and clusters of burials that shared characteristics (R. Joyce 1999b: 24–37). The distributional mapping of characteristics across the landscape of a site is a hybrid graphic form with both realistic representational aims and analytic goals. Its use in archaeology is most strongly associated with the exploration of the spatial location of activities, particularly in household archaeology (e.g., Kent 1987, 1990). As I summarized my results:

I found no evidence of strong associations among the entire suite of
objects included in burials. Instead, the burial assemblages may better
be viewed as composed of components included independently of one
another. The presence of any one of these components (for example,
figurines) does not provide clear grounds to expect other components.
A hierarchical structure of choice may, however, be discernible. Burials
with the rarest components usually also include more common components. Pottery vessels are most common and in many burials are the
only objects included. Each component can be viewed as an option
added to an initial common content, up to the rarest items: costume
worn by the deceased. Viewed as a structure of choice, the composition of Tlatilco burials most directly reflects the practices differently
employed by survivors belonging to different residential groups. . . .
The distributions of most of the features of burials are independent of
each other. The mortuary rituals that resulted in these distributions
combined different kinds of actions drawn from a suite of practices
common to the community as a whole. The use of pottery vessels in
mortuary rites throughout the community may reflect the importance
of meals in small-scale social relations between and within groups,
and the significance of pots as media for symbolism. Differentiation
between groups is most obvious in the choice to employ more variable
elements of burial preparation, such as red pigment. (R. Joyce 1999b:
23, 30)

By choosing to engage in this representation, I inflected my own
utterances about the creation of burials and clusters of burials at
Tlatilco as a form of activity analysis and as a response to dialogues
in household archaeology. I shifted my emphasis away from the essential social status of each buried person toward the activities through
which the dead came to rest where they were recorded by modern
archaeologists. I told a story different from that of the colleagues who
preceded me; not incompatible with it, but due to its different story-
line, attentive to different material remains.

Changing my own narrative interest in the same archaeological
materials, I subsequently produced another analysis, again in traditional form, whose differences can most simply be related to engagement in yet other archaeological dialogues (R. Joyce in press a). In
this version of my analysis, I again considered the possibility that
group membership was significant, but changed my focus from the
spatial clusters I had suggested represented household groups, to the
dispersed age cohorts whose members were buried in different locations. Here, I was concerned with how changes through the life cycle
of young women and men at Tlatilco affected their activities in life
and their social value to those who buried them. My major tools again

were statistical: summaries of frequencies of characteristics within different age ranges arrived at through exploratory data analysis. As I wrote:

> Elaborate costume was worn by young women between age 15 and 25, who were also accompanied by the largest number of other materials in their burials, including up to 11 figurines.... Older women, between 30 and 45 years old, not only wore less jewelry (at most a single strand of beads at the neck or wrist), but had only simple bone or shell beads and lacked the jade, rock crystal, and polished iron ore beads and pendants of the younger women.... Unique to these older women, however, was a high frequency of ceramic rattle balls, whose form and location in burials suggests they may have been worn on the legs, and of whistles that could have served as pendants. Five burials of women aged 25 to 40, three with no other imperishable costume ornaments, were accompanied by up to five rattles or whistles.
>
> The age range of men buried wearing costumes was slightly older than that of women, from 20 to 50, but again the most elaborate costumes were worn by younger men, those under 30. Among these were men who wore multiple strands of beads at neck, arm, and ankle, as well as ear spools and rings, incorporating jade, bone, shell, and iron ore. As with their young female counterparts, some males between 20 and 30 were buried with small ceramic masks and stamps that might be other media of beautification. Also like the women of Tlatilco, slightly older men, from age 25 to 35, were buried with up to three ceramic rattle balls. (R. Joyce in press a)

This account stood in dialogue not with mortuary or activity area analysis, but with archaeologies of subjectivity, including gender and age. The statistical summary of variations in burials was juxtaposed to a survey of representational conventions of contemporary figurines from Tlatilco. In response to studies by others of variation in representations of physical appearance in contemporary Mesoamerican figurines, my work on Tlatilco explicitly cited and revoiced these arguments (Cyphers Guillén 1993, Lesure 1997; compare R. Joyce 2000a).

Viewing the material remains in archaeological sites themselves as utterances by the past people who made and used them, it is possible to see the articles I wrote using my reanalysis of Tlatilco as dialogues not only with contemporary archaeological communities, using their distinct languages, but as dialogues with others in the past. Treating objects recovered archaeologically as anything like utterances has conventionally been equated with a concern with recovering of the intention of past actors to communicate. So it is important that I reiterate the Baktinian position taken here, and differentiate it from theories of communication more familiar in archaeology. To say that an object created by the inhabitants of Tlatilco around 1000 BC, recovered by an archaeologist in the late twentieth century, is an utterance is not to say that it was created with the intent of sending a message to anyone, least of all a person in a then-distant future. But it is to say that the object created was expressive, that it is a representation of, at the very least, a social engagement with the past world in which the people of Tlatilco lived. It is to say that objects recovered archaeologically are comparable to each other because they were manufactured by people engaged in dialogically seeking responses from those around them, and obtaining those responses, even if such a response was limited to making use of the object, and thus affirming it as recognizably useful (compare Shanks and Tilley 1987: 150–5, Tilley 1999: 269–72). To go further and view material actions in the past as representations, is to emphasize that representing is a an activity that occurs between different people. As Dan Sperber (1992: 59–61) argues, public representations can be traced epidemiologically, through their spread throughout communities, without the requirement of positing individual intentions. The evidence of the dialogic communication of utterances is present in the chain of their reproduction.

My task, then (and one I share with other archaeologists interested in trying to understand the experience of makers of the objects whose traces we follow in archaeological sites) is at least partly to respond to the objects produced in terms of their existence as unique entries in a dialogue, responses to prior material utterances (compare Cruikshank 2000: 98–115). I respond to the repetition of burial of young women with the largest number and variety of objects as a series of reiterations by the past inhabitants of Tlatilco of the social significance of young women. I respond to the exclusion in one neighborhood in the site of all but the most common of burial features as a refusal of participation in the community-wide dialogue of status and ceremony. I respond to the presence of iron-ore mirrors in only one burial in any cluster as an acceptance of a community-wide expression of value and an affirmative evaluation of the person singled out in each cluster. These are not overt forms of recognizing objects as representations, as would be my identification of certain figurines as images of youthful males and females. But they are responses to objects and patterns of objects as propositions by past actors, which I have a responsibility to evaluate, revoice, and to make a response.

"Objects do speak and should be heard as significant statements of personal and cultural reflexivity, as 'shapes that materialize a way of experiencing' and 'bring a particular cast of mind out into the world of objects'" (Babcock 1986: 318).

The form of my responses, the technical article, erases overt signs of my voice, but the article is a narrative distinguished by this specific form of voice (Harré 1990, Rose 1993: 205). I speak through a series of received languages, and tell stories about Tlatilco that are framed in narrative forms shaped by specific communities within archaeology. I treat the nonhuman material traces of past human action at Tlatilco as utterances and respond to them in my own words, evaluating their significance. I do so with a sideways glance toward the people I imagine as my readers, whose words I echo in pursuit of approval. I hope for a reader who will approve of my intentions, and shape my words for that super-addressee.

How far can such a process of narrativizing go? What experimental writers working in archaeology are proposing is that we take the materials we write about and rewrite them for multiple respondents. This process of writing and rewriting, telling and retelling, which as a discipline has been our history, today has the potential to create a space to engage beyond the disciplinary walls. It also has the power to create new knowledge as we reframe our understandings self-consciously at different scales, and in different space–time relationships.

This book ends with a re-presentation of the Tlatilco burial analysis, now in the form of a heteroglossic dialogue. The core of this work, presented at conferences as *Women of Tlatilco*, involves a deliberate move from the descriptive language of the standard field report to an emotional engagement with the loss, and the connection that survivors feel for the dead they bury (R. Joyce in press b). While the narrative is unconventional in its form, it conveys all the same information that the conventional presentation of the same material accomplishes, in an explicit story that houses multiple, irreducible voices.

Both fiction and science operate through a creation of metaphoric representations. The practices are by no means at war; both are fraught with a weight of responsibility. As William Gass (1970: 65) puts it:

> The scientist, after a time, finds himself with a store of observations of the natural world on the one hand, and a system of pure mathematical connections on the other. Within the mathematical system he can make inferences with great speed and accuracy. Unfortunately the system is

empty; it has no content; it tells him nothing about the world. His observations tell him nothing either, for logical connections cannot be perceived; his data remain disorganized; there are no paths through it for the mind. But if he decides to represent a body by a point and motion by a line, then the system becomes concrete, at once trapping a vast number of physical things in a web of logical relations.

7

Final Dialogues

Bodies Trapped in a Web of Relations

I treat the burials of women, not only because these have formed a major focus of my work on this population, but also because the very project I am undertaking greatly expands the space necessary to account for any one or few of the burials within the Tlatilco population.[12] An overall picture of women's lives at Tlatilco is easily summarized. The 86 female burials made up about 40 percent of the 212 excavated during the fourth excavation campaign (Garcia Moll, Juarez Cossio, Pijoan Aguade, M. E. Salas Cuesta, and M. Salas Cuesta 1991). They ranged in age from 15 to over 50 years old. Serious health problems included tooth decay (51 percent), noted as early as the age interval from 15 to 19 years, and arthritic degeneration of the spine, setting in as early as age 26 to 30 (19 percent). Perhaps as a result of infant and maternal mortality stemming from childbirth-related disease, 10 percent of the burials of females aged 20 through 44 included the bones of neonates. Around 77 percent of adult females (66) had tabular erect cranial deformation, a practice noted in unsexed skeletons beginning at nine months of age. But the composite female experience reflected here merges ages, as well as differences in elaboration between, and internal differentiation within, groups of burials likely to have been constructed by members of single social groups.

An alternative way of seeing the women in these burials looks at what we can say about the life of each one by viewing their treatment in death as a point in the trajectory of the creation of their own social identities and their memorialization by their survivors. In the following account, I move from a more traditional, scientific, and generalizing language to a more particularistic, experiential, and emotional language. I end with the imagined voice of one of the survivors of the events that resulted in the traces archaeologists uncovered at Tlatilco, as she remembered the people and happenings over her own lifetime. This latest attempt at a narrative for the women of Tlatilco enacts the reality that we have only fragments of past dialogues, and that these fragments may be, as Ruth Tringham suggests, better thought of as like memories or dreams of the past than as daylight visions seen from the all-knowing perspective of a viewer hovering in the sky. This narrative also responds to every earlier attempt, by myself and others, to tell a compelling story about the past. It is not through any one way of telling stories, but the cumulative effect of multiple narratives that the richness of past experience can possibly be hinted at in a responsible fashion.

> Burial 14A was one of five female burials forming a single cluster. Aged between 17 and 19 years, this individual exhibited the rarer tabular oblique cranial deformation, found in only seven burials at the site. The individual lacked any grave goods.
>
> The teenaged girl in burial 164 also was buried without any imperishable objects. Unlike the young woman in Burial 14A, her skull had been formed into the tabular erect shape more common among men and women at Tlatilco.
>
> The person in Burial 29, like Burial 164 the only female in her cluster, died at the same young age. Beginning in infancy her family had shaped her head to approximate their ideal of beauty, and at her young death, she had an elegantly swept-back forehead. Reflecting the wealth of her House and her access through it to the choicest foods, her teeth already showed signs of decay. Surviving members of her family placed with her a single bowl and figurine, the general offerings left with burials at Tlatilco, as well as a grinding stone and chipped stone scraper.
>
> The loss of the 19-year-old girl in burial 27 was felt deeply by her House. In life she had been intended to solidify ties between her House and another from the opposite sector of Tlatilco. Her mortuary ceremonies were elaborated by her House to establish her firmly in the memory of both groups. She was dressed in her fanciest costume, with pendants of jade, shell, and iron ore from the borders of Guatemala, along the Gulf Coast, and in the Oaxaca Valley, the distant ends of the world known to her House. Multiple bowls, bottles, and figurines were left in her grave as a sign of respect and of confidence that her death would not represent a permanent setback for her House.
>
> If all went well, the young woman of burial 27 might one day be remembered as an important ancestor, like the two teenage girls whose skulls were gathered with those of two other, older women in a pit in the courtyard of a neighboring house. The older of these two girls was

accompanied in this relocation by the mandible of her six-month-old child, whose birth had ended her life and in turn, through her death, his own.

Childbirth constituted a major risk for the younger adult women of the settlement, who often went to the grave with the bodies of their own newborn infants. The 24-year-old woman in Burial 208 was part of a large, if not wealthy, House, one of eight women buried in the compound. Like all the women of her House her head had carefully been shaped to enhance her appearance. She had little access to rare foods, the prerogative of the elder women of her group. But in death her House, never able to afford much mortuary display, provided her with multiple pottery vessels and figurines as a sign of respect to the House of the father of the child she died bearing, whose body was placed in the ground with her. With luck other women of the House might cement the bonds that had begun with this marriage, and help to increase the power and resources of the House.

Such strategies had worked for the Houses to the east, whose alliances with distant villages provided abundant exotic goods, and whose ability to retain married children and their offspring provided enough labor to support House members skilled in producing obsidian blades and elaborate cotton textiles. When a daughter of one of these houses died in full youth, like the woman in Burial 95, she could be buried with elaborate mortuary ritual attended by all the other Houses to which her own was allied, because her House had the wealth necessary for display, feasting, and hospitality. The beauty of her artificially shaped head, elaborately dressed hair, and young body was further enhanced with shell, jade, and iron-ore beads and pendants, and red pigment sprinkled over her. Nineteen pots and 10 figurines were dedicated to her burial, including some of the most elaborate in the village. In recognition of the importance of obsidian working in the history of her House, a single flake and a bone punch were added to the grave. Although young to die, at 24, her mortuary rituals further cemented the ties to her husband's House already forged over several generations.

The rites accompanying the interment of her slightly older House sister in burial 109 were more modest, befitting her less untimely death and the lesser risk it posed to House alliances. Nevertheless, the House took care to mark her burial with the same signs of its history, bone punches and an obsidian core, and placed an animal mandible ornament to complement her beautifully shaped skull and finely filed teeth. She had already achieved an honored place in life, and the beginnings of decay in her teeth reflected the access she had enjoyed to sweet foods. The two pots placed with the body were the minimum required for the ceremony, but well made and no insult to the House to which she had borne children.

When necessary, the House invested more in the burial of a daughter who died at the brink of old age. The 39-year-old woman in Burial
130 was relatively healthy, despite the tooth decay she owed to the
wealth of her House and her honored status within it. Her death, while
not unusually early, was sooner than that of other women in the community, and she left behind a large number of children and grandchil-
dren to mourn her. These descendants saw that she was accompanied
by two dozen of the finest pots, and five figurines, and carefully placed
her grinding stones in the burial. They dressed her in the clay rattles
that she wore when, with the other mothers, she danced in recollection
of her youth.

In this, she was like the older woman of the western House, placed
in Burial 157 accompanied by 21 pots and four whistles, wearing bone
bead ornaments and her rattles. While the wealth of her House was
less, and it lacked the wide external connections and active trading part-
nerships of the southeast House, it was equally proud of its history and
respectful of the women who helped distinguish it from lesser neighboring Houses.

For most women in their late thirties, life was difficult and death
was little marked. The women in Burials 105 and 115 were respectfully
buried by the surviving members of their House, one with three pots,
the other wearing shell beads and her rattle ornaments. But both had
already, by age 39, suffered serious spinal arthritis and tooth decay; the
woman in Burial 105 had lesions on her jaw as well. While the House
managed to mark the burials of younger women, on whom their
alliances depended, with appropriate offerings of up to 20 pots and 11
figurines, and ornaments of shell and iron ore, it was not large enough
to spare its elder women the hard labor that gradually deformed their
spines and crippled their bodies.

Some singularly important women over 40 were given prominent,
isolated burials by the groups of Houses who recognized debts to
them. The older woman in Burial 9 was covered in red pigment like a
much younger girl, had her stone pestle at her hand, and two dogs were
killed to accompany her after death. She had practiced her craft of div-
ination and curing for the village as a whole, and was no longer counted
a member of an individual House. The skull of another older woman
was recovered, burned, and placed in Burial 182 along with a single pot
and a basalt yoke, emblem of the ritual ballgame through which her
head was identified with the sprouting seed of the underworld tree of
life. No longer identified as a named person, she stood as a generalized
representative of the founding ancestors venerated by the Houses of
the southeastern neighborhood, who had promised and delivered the
knowledge of working obsidian to their descendants.

But most elderly women were buried more simply. The 44-year-old
woman in Burial 189 wore a simple necklace of bone beads. The 50-

year-old woman in Burial 195 in the same group was placed in her grave
with no imperishable ornamentation at all, and like her House sister
had no pottery vessels or figurines in her grave. The extremely elderly
woman in Burial 63, bent by severe spinal arthritis, although sufficiently well loved to be carefully buried was also placed in her grave
without ornament or elaboration. Unlike the younger women of
Tlatilco, these older women had established their social memories
through their lives, and through the names of their children and children's children. No post-mortem construction of a history was needed
for them.

Revoicing the Dead at Tlatilco

Tomorrow we will bury you, my elder sister. We have dressed you in
all the finery we have to offer: shell beads from the ocean, white and
red, like bone and blood, and jade beads, bright green like the first
shoots of plants after the rains come again. There is a mirror waiting
to be placed on your body, polished, gleaming, dark and light at once.
I hear the elders murmuring among themselves as they prepare the
food for our guests, our brothers' families, who have come from all
the towns within reach of this news. All day today I ground the red
pigment to spread over you when we place you below the patio floor.
I am so tired, but I do not want to sleep, because after tomorrow I
will only see your beautiful face in my memory. . . .

She is in the earth now. I can remember her teaching me to press
away the tiny flakes of obsidian, as you did, our mothers and fathers,
the first of our House to use the black stone. At her graveside, I
honored her, I honored you, using my bone punch to make the flakes
needed for the ceremony. At the end, I placed the last one with her, I
gave her my prized bone punch, I sent them with her on the journey
to join you. . . .

You do not remember her. You were too young; some of you
were not with us yet. She was beautiful when the elder sisters danced,
the mothers beating out the rhythm with their rattles, their beads
glimmering. She outshone them all. She would stand, dressed in
her beads, red, white, green, shimmering iron ore mirror around
her neck, and as she whirled, her skirt would spin out, the painted
markings on her body would flash in and out of the light of the fire.
Imagine the figurines of dancers, but not as you see them all at once;
imagine them whirling, just like the young girls do today, so that a
shoulder, an ear, a cheek, the sloping forehead with its beautifully

shaved hair, comes in and out of view. The echoes of the songs crashed like waves. . . .

My sleep is troubled. In my dream the houses are gone, we are not here, no one knows our names. Will there be anyone to hold this obsidian flake that I use to carve this small figure of my long-dead sister? Will there be anyone to admire her hair, her mirror, her pose as she launches into the dance? Even now, I can hardly remember her face, only the image of all the young girls. . . .

Notes

1   This dialogue is reproduced as originally written. Because neither of the authors are at the email addresses they occupied in 1994, the former email addresses have been blanked out. Minor typographic errors in the original have been amended as well.

2   See Conkey (1978), Conkey and Williams (1991), Gero (1983, 1985, 1991a, 1991b: 166–9, 1991c), R. Joyce (1994), Preucel and Chesson (1994). Other essays in Claassen (1994), Nelson, Nelson and Wylie (1994), and Reyman (1992), and especially Levine (1991, 1994, 1999) contribute to the history of women's involvement in archaeology in North America; compare Zeder (1997), Yellen (1983, 1991).

3   See Haraway (1983, 1989, 1991); compare Landau (1991).

4   See, for example, Shanks (1992).

5   Propp (1968).

6   See Arbib and Hesse (1986: 156).

7   This chapter, with the exception of the opening epigraph and endnotes, was composed by Jeanne Lopiparo as a commentary on the rationale for her as-yet-unpublished multimedia computer hypertext project *Crafting Cosmos*. As she notes, there is an inherent difficulty in trying to write in linear print about nonlinear, nonprint media. In this chapter, sources available through hypertext links in the original cannot be accessed from the linear text figures. In Figure 4.9, quotations are from Gossen and Leventhal (1993: 211, 212). In Figures 10 and 11, quotations are from Gossen (1974: 199). In Figure 4.15, the source quoted is Rice (1998: 242). The future of archaeology is not in print; it is in the new media, and thinking through their implications now will be crucial (McDavid 1999, Tringham 1998). See chapter 5 for more discussion of this point. Lopiparo also takes up the issue of treating material culture as text (compare Hodder 1986, 1989a, 1999: 66–79, Tilley 1999), or, following Bakhtin, as utterance.

8   There are two constraints at present on designing hypermedia for the World Wide Web. One of these is that doing so can introduce limitations of available linking technologies, considerably reducing the density of hypertextual effects. The other is the pragmatic one of pro-

viding access to complex projects, such as *Crafting Cosmos*, that incorporate sound and motion, without creating inequities in access based on bandwidth and speed of connection. The program at the University of California, Berkeley initiated by Ruth Tringham (MACTiA, the Multimedia Authoring Center for Teaching in Anthropology; http://www.mactia.berkeley.edu), through which Lopiparo developed *Crafting Cosmos*, began with an orientation toward producing richer, free-standing computer multimedia projects. The faculty and teaching assistants of MACTiA (including Lopiparo and Joyce) are now training students to develop their projects for the Web as well, so that they understand the limitations and possibilities of both platforms.

9   *Sister Stories* was published online in December, 2000, by New York University Press. Because it was originally created as a stand-alone hypertext in *Storyspace*, publication on the Web required complete redesign, which was carried out by Carolyn Guyer. The NYU Press version has 303 html pages, 200 images, and more than 600 links. As is evident, one of the costs of translation from one medium to the other is a loss of the dense links that grew out of the original collaboration. Equally obvious is the extraordinary growth of graphics in the Web version. True to the Bakhtinian spirit of this book, I retain my discussion of a previous utterance of *Sister Stories*, and invite readers to listen to the new echoes of the work online.

10 This is a transcription of one possible reading of the final *Storyspace* version of *Sister Stories*. It presents only a fraction of the kinds of texts included in the original. While selected to illustrate specific points, this transcription is truthful; someone using the computerized hypertext could trace precisely this route through it. The linked phrase which was selected to make each connection is indicated by underlining. If no phrase is underlined, the choice was a default for the entire passage. Some deletion of text was required to keep this a manageable length; deletions are indicated using the email convention for deleted material: ⟨. . .⟩. In the ideal world, this section and the following one, which comments on the reading, would be set parallel to each other so you could read both in juxtaposition (compare Shanks 1995).

Due to the process of adaptation for publication on the Web, it is not possible to follow precisely this path in the on-line published edition. I have added the html links for the specific pages in the on-line edition that correspond to these text fragments; in the spirit of nonlinearity, readers are welcome to enter the text at any of these points.

11 "Mind your manners. When authorship is proffered, refuse it; when authorship is generalized, claim its particularity. If they say you're an author, refuse to be; if they say everyone's an author, tell them your name is Willa or Edna" (M. Joyce 1995: 131).

12 This section rewrites some of the material presented in R. Joyce (in press b). The final section in this chapter is entirely new.

Bibliography

Allison, P. 1999: Labels for ladles: Interpreting material culture of Roman households. In P. Allison (ed.), *The Archaeology of Household Activities*, London: Routledge, 57–77.

Appadurai, A. 1986: Introduction: Commodities and the politics of value. In A. Appadurai (ed.), *The Social Life of Things: Commodities in Cultural Perspective*, Cambridge: Cambridge University Press, 3–63.

Arbib, M. A. and Hesse, M. B. 1986: *The Construction of Reality*. Cambridge: Cambridge University Press.

Arnold, B. 1990: Past as propaganda: Totalitarian archaeology in Nazi Germany. *Antiquity* 64, 464–78.

Arvey, M. 1988: Women of ill-repute in the Florentine Codex. In V. E. Miller (ed.), *The Role of Gender in Precolumbian Art and Architecture*, Lanham, MD: University Press of America, 179–204.

Atkinson, R. J. C. 1946: *Field Archaeology*. London: Methuen.

Babcock, B. 1986: Modeled selves: Helen Codere's "Little People." In V. W. Turner and E. M. Bruner (eds), *The Anthropology of Experience*, Urbana: University of Illinois Press, 316–43.

Baigrie, B. (ed.) 1996: *Picturing Knowledge: Historical and Philosophical Problems Concerning the Use of Art in Science*. Toronto: University of Toronto Press.

Baker, F. 1989: Making producers out of consumers: Archaeology and the media into the 1990s. *Archaeological Review from Cambridge* 8, 234–8.

Baker, F., Taylor, S., and Thomas, J. 1990: Writing the past in the present: An introductory dialogue. In F. Baker, S. Taylor, and J. Thomas (eds), *Writing the Past in the Present*, Lampeter: St. David's University College, 1–11.

Bakhtin, M. M. 1981: *The Dialogic Imagination: Four Essays*. C. Emerson and M. Holquist (trs), M. Holquist (ed.). Austin: University of Texas Press.

———1984: *Problems of Dostoevsky's Poetics*. C. Emerson (tr. and ed.). Minneapolis: University of Minnesota Press.

———1986: *Speech Genres and Other Late Essays*. V. W. McGee (tr.), C. Emerson and M. Holquist (eds). Austin: University of Texas Press.

——1990: *Art and Answerability: Early Philosophical Essays by M. M. Bakhtin*. V. Liapunov and K. Brostrom (trs), M. Holquist and V. Liapunov (eds). Austin: University of Texas Press.

——1993: *Toward a Philosophy of the Act*. V. Liapunov (tr.), V. Liapunov and M. Holquist (eds). Austin: University of Texas Press.

Bapty, I. 1989: The Meanings of Things, writing, and archaeology. *Archaeological Review from Cambridge* 8, 175–84.

——1990: The agony and the ecstasy: The emotions of writing the past, a tragedy in one act for three voices. *Archaeological Review from Cambridge* 9, 233–42.

Barthes, R. 1972: *Mythologies*. A. Lavers (tr.). London: Jonathan Cape.

——1975: *S/Z*. R. Miller (tr.). London: Jonathan Cape.

——1977a: The death of the author. In *Image–Music–Text*, S. Heath (tr.). New York: Noonday Press, 142–8.

——1977b: Diderot, Brecht, Eisenstein. In *Image–Music–Text*. S. Heath (tr.), New York: Noonday Press, 69–78.

——1977c: Introduction to the structural analysis of narratives. In *Image–Music–Text*. S. Heath (tr.), New York: Noonday Press, 79–124.

——1977d: Rhetoric of the image. In *Image–Music–Text*. S. Heath (tr.), New York: Noonday Press, 32–51.

——1981: The discourse of history. S. Bann (tr.), *Comparative Criticism*, 3, 7–20.

——1990: *The Fashion System*, M. Ward and R. Howard (tr.). Berkeley: University of California Press.

Beaudry, M. C. 1998: Farm journal: first person, four voices. *Historical Archaeology* 32, 20–33.

Beaudry, M. C. and White, J. 1994: Cowgirls with the blues? A study of women's publication and the citation of women's work in *Historical Archaeology*. In C. Claassen (ed.), *Women in Archaeology*, Philadelphia: University of Pennsylvania Press, 138–58.

Behar, R. and Gordon, D. A. (eds) 1995: *Women Writing Culture*. Berkeley: University of California Press.

Bender, B. 1998: *Stonehenge: Making Space*. Oxford: Berg.

Billig, M. 1993: Psychology, rhetoric and cognition. In R. H. Roberts and J. M. M. Good (eds), *The Recovery of Rhetoric: Persuasive Discourse and Disciplinarity in the Human Sciences*, Charlottesville: University Press of Virginia, 119–36.

Binford, L. 1968: Archeological perspectives. In S. R. Binford and L. R. Binford (eds), *New Perspectives in Archeology*, Chicago: Aldine, 5–32.

Boivin, N. 1997: Insidious or just boring? An examination of academic writing in archaeology. *Archaeological Review from Cambridge* 14, 105–25.

Bolter, J. D. 1991: *Writing Space: The Computer, Hypertext, and the History of Writing*. Hillsdale, NJ: Lawrence Erlbaum and Associates.

Bourdieu, P. 1973: The Berber House. In M. Douglas (ed.), *Rules and Meanings: The Anthropology of Everyday Knowledge*, Harmondsworth: Penguin Books, 98–110.

———1977: *Outline of a Theory of Practice*. R. Nice (tr.). Cambridge: Cambridge University Press.

Bradley, R. 1997: "To see is to have seen": Craft traditions in British field archaeology. In B. Molyneaux (ed.), *The Cultural Life of Images: Visual Representation in Archaeology*, London: Routledge, 62–72.

Brown, B. A. 1983: Seen but not heard: Women in Aztec ritual – the Sahagún texts. In J. C. Berlo (ed.), *Text and Image in Pre-Columbian Art*, Oxford: BAR International Series 180, 119–54.

Brown, C., Beck, W., Murphy, D., Perkins, T., Smith, A., and Somerville, M. 2000: *The Old Camp: Corindi Lake North*. University of New England and Yarrawarra Aboriginal Corporation.

Brumfiel, E. 1996: Figurines and the Aztec state: Testing the effectiveness of ideological dominance. In R. P. Wright (ed.), *Gender and Archaeology*, Philadelphia: University of Pennsylvania Press, 143–66.

Burshatin, I. 1996: Elena alias Eleno: Genders, sexualities, and "race" in the mirror of natural history in sixteenth-century Spain. In S. P. Ramet (ed.), *Gender Reversals and Gender Cultures: Anthropological and Historical Perspectives*, London and New York: Routledge, 105–22.

Butler, J. 1999: A "Bad Writer" Bites Back. *The New York Times*, March 20, Op-Ed page.

Claassen, C. (ed.) 1994: *Women in Archaeology*. Philadelphia: University of Pennsylvania Press.

Clark, J. E. and Parry, W. 1990: Craft specialization and cultural complexity. *Research in Economic Anthropology* 12, 289–346.

Clifford, J. 1983: On ethnographic authority. *Representations* 1, 118–46.

———1986: Introduction: Partial truths. In J. Clifford and G. E. Marcus (eds), *Writing Culture: The Poetics and Politics of Ethnography*, Berkeley: University of California Press, 1–26.

Clifford, J. and Marcus, G. (eds) 1986: *Writing Culture: The Poetics and Politics of Ethnography*. Berkeley: University of California Press.

Conkey, M. W. 1978: Getting grants: Participation of women in the research process. Paper presented at the Annual Meeting of the American Anthropological Association, Los Angeles.

Conkey, M. W. and Tringham, R. E. 1996: Archaeology and the Goddess: Exploring the contours of feminist archaeology. In A. Stewart and D. Stanton (eds), *Feminisms in the Academy: Rethinking the Disciplines*, Ann Arbor: University of Michigan Press, 199–247.

Conkey, M. W. and Williams, S. 1991: Original narratives: The political economy of gender in archaeology. In M. di Leonardo (ed.), *Gender at the Crossroads of Knowledge: Feminist Anthropology in the Postmodern Era*, Berkeley: University of California Press, 102–39.

Connerton, P. 1989: *How Societies Remember*. Cambridge: Cambridge University Press.

Costello, J. G. 1998: Bread fresh from the oven: Memories of Italian bread-baking in the California mother-lode. *Historical Archaeology* 32, 66–73.

———2000: *Red Light Voices*: An archaeological drama of late nineteenth-century prostitution. In R. A. Schmidt and B. L. Voss (eds), *Archaeologies of Sexuality*, London: Routledge, 160–75.

Costin, C. 1991: Craft specialization: Issues in defining, documenting, and explaining the organization of production. *Archaeological Method and Theory* 3, 1–56.

Cruikshank, J. 2000: *The Social Life of Stories: Narrative and Knowledge in the Yukon Territory*. Lincoln: University of Nebraska Press.

Cyphers Guillén, A. 1993: Women, rituals, and social dynamics at ancient Chalcatzingo. *Latin American Antiquity* 4, 209–24.

Danow, D. K. 1991: *The Thought of Mikhail Bakhtin: From Word to Culture*. New York: St. Martin's Press.

Daviss, B. 1997: Simple art of survival. *New Scientist* 154 (2086), 38–41.

Deetz, J. 1988: History and archaeological theory: Walter Taylor revisited. *American Antiquity* 53, 13–22.

———1989: Archaeography, archaeology or archeology? *American Journal of Archaeology* 93, 429–35.

———1998: Discussion: Archaeologists as storytellers. *Historical Archaeology* 32, 94–6.

De Cunzo, L. A. 1998: A future after freedom. *Historical Archaeology* 32, 42–54.

Deleuze, G. and Guattari, F. 1988: *A Thousand Plateaus: Capitalism and Schizophrenia*. Minneapolis: University of Minnesota Press.

Deloria, Jr., V. 1992: Indians, archaeologists and the future. *American Antiquity* 57, 595–8.

Donley-Reid, L. W. 1990: A structuring structure: The Swahili house. In S. Kent (ed.), *Domestic Architecture and the Use of Space: An Interdisciplinary Cross-Cultural Study*, Cambridge: Cambridge University Press, 114–26.

Edmonson, M. (ed.) 1974: *Sixteenth-Century Mexico: The Work of Sahagún*. Albuquerque: University of New Mexico Press.

Fabian, J. 1991: Of dogs alive, birds dead, and time to tell a story. In J. Bender and D. E. Wellbery (eds), *Chronotypes: The Construction of Time*, Stanford: Stanford University Press, 185–204.

Flannery, K. V. (ed.) 1976: *The Early Mesoamerican Village*. Academic Press: New York.

Fotiadis, M. 1992: Units of data as deployment of disciplinary codes. In J.-C. Gardin and C. S. Peebles (eds), *Representations in Archaeology*, Bloomington: Indiana University Press, 132–48.

Fritz, J. and Plog, F. 1970: The nature of archaeological explanation. *American Antiquity* 35, 405–12.

Galloway, P. 1992: The unexamined habitus: Direct historic analogy and the archaeology of the text. In J.-C. Gardin and C. S. Peebles (eds),

Representations in Archaeology, Bloomington: Indiana University Press, 178–95.

Garcia Moll, R., Juarez Cossio, D., Pijoan Aguade, C., Salas Cuesta, M. E., and Salas Cuesta, M. 1991: *Catálogo de Entierros de San Luis Tlatilco, México, Temporada IV*. Mexico, DF: Instituto Nacional de Antropología e Historia, Serie Antropología Física-Arqueología.

Gardin, J.-C. 1992: Semiotic trends in archaeology. In J.-C. Gardin and C. S. Peebles (eds), *Representations in Archaeology*, Bloomington: Indiana University Press, 86–104.

Gass, W. H. 1970: *Fiction and the Figures of Life*. New York: Knopf.

Geertz, C. 1973: Thick Description: Toward an interpretive theory of culture. In *The Interpretation of Cultures: Selected Essays*, New York: Basic Books, 3–31.

Genette, G. 1980: *Narrative Discourse: An Essay in Method*. J. E. Lewin (tr.). Ithaca: Cornell University Press.

——— 1988: *Narrative Discourse Revisited*. J. E. Lewin (tr.). Ithaca: Cornell University Press.

Gero, J. 1983: Gender bias in archaeology: A cross-cultural perspective. In J. Gero, D. Lacy, and M. Blakey (eds), *The Socio-Politics of Archaeology*, Department of Anthropology, Research Report No. 23, Amherst, MA: Department of Anthropology, University of Massachusetts, 51–7.

——— 1985: Socio-politics of archaeology and the woman-at-home ideology. *American Antiquity* 50, 342–50.

——— 1991a: Gender divisions of labor in the construction of archaeological knowledge. In D. Walde and N. Willows (eds), *The Archaeology of Gender*, Proceedings of the 22nd Annual Chac Mool Conference, Calgary: Archaeological Association, University of Calgary, 96–102.

——— 1991b: Genderlithics: Women's roles in stone tool production. In J. Gero and M. Conkey (eds), *Engendering Archaeology: Women and Prehistory*, Oxford: Basil Blackwell, 163–93.

——— 1991c: The social world of prehistoric facts: Gender and power in Paleoindian research. In H. du Cros and L. Smith (eds), *Women in Archaeology: A Feminist Critique*, Occasional Papers in Archaeology, No. 23, Canberra: Department of Prehistory, Research School of Pacific Studies, Australian National University, 31–40.

——— 1996: Archeological practice and gendered encounters with field data. In R. P. Wright (ed.), *Gender and Archaeology*, Philadelphia: University of Pennsylvania Press, 251–80.

Giddens, A. 1979: *Central Problems in Social Theory: Action, Structure and Contradiction in Social Analysis*. Berkeley: University of California Press.

——— 1981: *A Contemporary Critique of Historical Materialism*. Berkeley: University of California Press.

——— 1984: *The Constitution of Society: Outline of a Theory of Structuration*. Berkeley: University of California Press.

Gillespie, S. D. 1989: *The Aztec Kings: The Construction of Rulership in Mexica History*. Tucson: University of Arizona Press.

——2000a: Beyond kinship: An introduction. In R. A. Joyce and S. D. Gillespie (eds), *Beyond Kinship: Social and Material Reproduction in House Societies*, Philadelphia: University of Pennsylvania Press, 1–21.

——2000b: Maya "Nested Houses": The Ritual Construction of Place. In R. A. Joyce and S. D. Gillespie (eds), *Beyond Kinship: Social and Material Reproduction in House Societies*, Philadelphia: University of Pennsylvania Press, 135–60.

Givens, D. R. 1992: The role of biography in writing the history of archaeology. In J. Reyman (ed.), *Rediscovering Our Past: Essays on the History of American Archaeology*, Aldershot: Avebury, 51–6.

Gossen, G. H. 1974: *Chamulas in the World of the Sun: Time and Space in the Maya Oral Tradition*. Cambridge, MA: Harvard University Press.

Gossen, G. H. and Leventhal, R. M. 1993: Topography of ancient Maya religious pluralism: a dialogue with the present. In J. A. Sabloff and J. S. Henderson (eds), *Lowland Maya Civilization in the Eighth Century A. D.*, Washington, DC: Dumbarton Oaks Research Library and Collection, 185–217.

Guyer, C. 1992: Buzz-Daze jazz and the quotidian stream. Presented in the session "Hypertext, Hypermedia: Defining a Fictional Form" at the annual meeting of the Modern Language Association, New York.

——1996: Fretwork: ReForming me. *Readerly/Writerly Texts*, Spring 1996.

Guyer, C. and Petry, M. 1991: Notes for *Izme Pass* exposé. *Writing on the Edge* 2 (2). Davis: University of California.

Hamilton, N. 2000: The conceptual archive and the challenge of gender. In I. Hodder (ed.), *Towards a Reflexive Method in Archaeology: The Example at Çatalhöyük*, British Institute of Archaeology at Ankara Monograph No. 28, Cambridge: McDonald Institute for Archaeological Research, 95–9.

Haraway, D. 1983: Primatology is politics by other means: Women's place is in the jungle. In R. Blier (ed.), *Feminist Approaches to Science*, New York: Pergamon, 77–118.

——1989: *Primate Visions: Gender, Race and Nature in the World of Modern Science*. New York: Routledge.

——1991: Situated knowledges: The science question in feminism and the privilege of partial perspective. In *Simians, Cyborgs and Women: The Reinvention of Nature*. New York: Routledge, 183–201.

Harding, S. 1991: *Whose Science? Whose Knowledge? Thinking from Women's Lives*. Ithaca: Cornell University Press.

Harré, R. 1990: Some Narrative Conventions of Scientific Discourse. In C. Nash (ed.), *Narrative in Culture: The Uses of Storytelling in the Sciences, Philosophy, and Literature*, London: Routledge, 81–101.

Henderson, J. S. and Joyce, R. A. In press: Puerto Escondido: Exploraciones preliminares del Formativo Temprano. *Yaxkin*.

Hendon, J. A. 1991: Status and power in Classic Maya society: An archeological study. *American Anthropologist* 93, 894–918.

———1999: The Pre-Classic Maya compound as the focus of social identity. In D. C. Grove and R. A. Joyce (eds), *Social Patterns in Pre-Classic Mesamerica*, Washington, DC: Dumbarton Oaks Research Library and Collection, 97–125.

———2000: Having and holding: Storage, memory, knowledge, and social relations. *American Anthropologist* 102, 42–53.

Hendon, J. A. and Lopiparo, J. In press: Investigaciones recientes en Cerro Palenque, Cortés, Honduras. *Yaxkin*.

Herzfeld, M. 1992: Metapatterns: Archaeology and the uses of evidential scarcity. In J.-C. Gardin and C. S. Peebles (eds), *Representations in Archaeology*, Bloomington: Indiana University Press, 66–86.

Hill, J. 1995: The voices of Don Gabriel: Responsibility and self in a modern Mexicano narrative. In D. Tedlock and B. Mannheim (eds), *The Dialogic Emergence of Culture*, Urbana: University of Illinois Press, 97–147.

Hodder, I. 1986: *Reading the Past: Current Approaches to Interpretation in Archaeology*. Cambridge: Cambridge University Press.

———1987: The meaning of discard: Ash and domestic space in Baringo. In S. Kent (ed.), *Method and Theory For Activity Area Research: An Ethnoarchaeological Approach*, New York: Columbia University Press, 424–48.

———1989a: This is not an article about material culture as text. *Journal of Anthropological Archaeology* 8, 250–69.

———1989b: Writing archaeology. *Antiquity* 63, 268–74.

———1992: Towards radical doubt: A dialogue. *Theory and Practice in Archaeology*. London: Routledge, 155–9.

———1993: Narrative and rhetoric of material culture sequences. *World Archaeology* 25, 268–82.

———1995: Material culture in time. In I. Hodder, M. Shanks, A. Alexandri, V. Buchli, J. Carman, J. Last, and G. Lucas (eds), *Interpreting Archaeology: Finding Meaning in the Past*, London: Routledge, 164–8.

———1997: "Always momentary, fluid and flexible": Towards a reflexive excavation methodology. *Antiquity* 71, 691–700.

———1999: *The Archaeological Process: An Introduction*. Oxford: Blackwell.

———2000: Part A: The integration of methods. In I. Hodder (ed.), *Towards a Reflexive Method in Archaeology: The Example at Çatalhöyük*, British Institute of Archaeology at Ankara Monograph No. 28, Cambridge: McDonald Institute for Archaeological Research, 16–18.

Holquist, M. 1990: *Dialogism: Bakhtin and his World*. London: Routledge.

James, S. 1997: Drawing inferences: Visual reconstructions in theory and practice. In B. Molyneaux (ed.), *The Cultural Life of Images: Visual Representation in Archaeology*, London: Routledge, 22–48.

Jefferson, A. 1989: Bodymatters: Self and Other in Bakhtin, Sartre and Barthes. In K. Hirschkop and D. Shepherd (eds), *Bakhtin and Cultural Theory*, Manchester: Manchester University Press.

Johnson, M. 1999: *Archaeological Theory: An Introduction*. Oxford: Blackwell.

Joyce, M. 1995: *Of Two Minds: Hypertext Pedagogy and Poetics*. Ann Arbor: University of Michigan Press.

———2000: One story: Present tense spaces of the heart. In *Othermindedness: The Emergence of Network Culture*, Ann Arbor: University of Michigan Press, 123–30.

Joyce, R. A. 1988: The Ulúa Valley and the coastal Maya lowlands: The View from Cerro Palenque. In G. R. Willey and E. Boone (eds), *The Southeast Classic Maya Zone*, Washington, DC: Dumbarton Oaks Research Library and Collection, 269–95.

———1991: *Cerro Palenque: Power and Identity on the Maya Periphery*. Austin: University of Texas Press.

———1992a: Classic Maya images of gender and labor. In C. Claassen (ed.), *Exploring Gender Through Archaeology: Selected Papers from the 1991 Boone Conference*, Monographs in World Archaeology, No. 11, Madison, WI: Prehistory Press, 63–70.

———1992b: Ideology and action: Classic Maya ritual practice. In S. Goldsmith, S. Garvie, D. Selin, and J. Smith (eds), *Ancient Images, Ancient Thought: The Archaeology of Ideology*, Proceedings, Chacmool Annual Conference no. 23, Calgary: Calgary Archaeological Association, 497–505.

———1992c: Innovation, communication and the archaeological record: A reassessment of Middle Formative Honduras. *Journal of the Steward Anthropological Society* 20, 235–56.

———1993a: The construction of the Maya Periphery and the Mayoid image of Honduran polychrome ceramics. In M. M. Graham (ed.), *Reinterpreting Prehistory of Central America*, Niwot: University of Colorado Press, 51–101.

———1993b: Women's work: Images of production and reproduction in prehispanic southern Central America. *Current Anthropology* 34, 255–74.

———1994: Dorothy Hughes Popenoe: Eve in an archaeological garden. In C. Claassen (ed.), *Women in Archaeology*, Philadelphia: University of Pennsylvania Press, 51–66.

———1996a: The construction of gender in Classic Maya monuments. In R. P. Wright (ed.), *Gender and Archaeology*, Philadelphia: University of Pennsylvania Press, 167–95.

———1996b: Social dynamics of exchange: Changing patterns in the Honduran archaeological record. In C. H. Langebaek and F. Cardenas-Arroyo (eds), *Chieftains, Power and Trade: Regional Interaction in the Intermediate Area of the Americas*, Bogotá, Colombia: Departamento de Antropología, Universidad de los Andes, 31–46.

———1998a: Performing the body in Pre-Hispanic Central America. *Res* 33, 147–66.

———1998b: Telling stories. Paper prepared for the SAR Advanced Seminar "Doing Archaeology as a Feminist." Margaret Conkey and Alison Wylie, organizers. Santa Fe, NM: School of American Research.

———1999a: Academic freedom, stewardship, and cultural heritage: Weighing the interests of stakeholders in crafting repatriation approaches. Keynote address, World Archaeological Congress 4, Cape Town: South Africa.

———1999b: Social dimensions of Pre-Classic burials. In D. C. Grove and R. A. Joyce (eds), *Social Patterns in Pre-Classic Mesamerica*, Washington, DC: Dumbarton Oaks Research Library and Collection, 15–48.

———2000a: Girling the girl and boying the boy: The production of adulthood in ancient Mesoamerica. *World Archaeology* 31, 473–83.

———2000b: Heirlooms and houses: Materiality and social memory. In R. A. Joyce and S. D. Gillespie (eds), *Beyond Kinship: Social and Material Reproduction in House Societies*, Philadelphia: University of Pennsylvania Press, 189–212.

———In press a: Beauty, sexuality, body ornamentation and gender in ancient Mesoamerica. In S. Nelson (ed.), *In Pursuit of Gender*, Walnut Creek, CA: AltaMira Press.

———In press b: Burying the dead at Tlatilco: Social memory and social identities. In M. Chesson (ed.), *New Perspectives on Mortuary Analysis*, Washington, DC: American Anthropological Association, Archeology Division, Archeology Papers No. 10.

Joyce, R. A. and Gillespie, S. D. (eds) 2000: *Beyond Kinship: Social and Material Reproduction in House Societies*. Philadelphia: University of Pennsylvania Press.

Joyce, R. A., Guyer, C., and Joyce, M. 2000: *Sister Stories*. http://www.nyupress.nyu.edu/sisterstories. New York: New York University Press.

Joyce, R. A. and Henderson, J. S. 2001: Beginnings of village life in eastern Mesoamerica. *Latin American Antiquity* 12, 5–24.

Joyce, R. A. and Hendon, J. A. 2000: Heterarchy, history, and material reality: "Communities" in Late Classic Honduras. In M.-A. Canuto and J. Yaeger (eds), *The Archaeology of Communities: A New World Perspective*, London: Routledge, 143–59.

Kent, S. (ed.) 1987: *Method and Theory For Activity Area Research: An Ethnoarchaeological Approach*. New York: Columbia University Press.

———1990: *Domestic Architecture and the Use of Space: An Interdisciplinary Cross-Cultural Study*. Cambridge: Cambridge University Press.

Klein, C. 1993: Shield women: resolution of an Aztec gender paradox. In A. Cordy-Collins and D. Sharon (eds), *Current Topics in Aztec Studies: Essays in Honor of Dr. H. B. Nicholson*, San Diego: San Diego Museum of Man, Papers vol. 30, 39–64.

————1994: Fighting with femininity: Gender and war in Aztec Mexico. *Estudios de Cultura Nahuatl* 24, 219–53.

Klor de Alva, J. J., Nicholson, H. B., and Quiñones Keber, E. (eds) 1988: *The Work of Bernardino de Sahagún: Pioneer Ethnographer of Sixteenth-century Aztec Mexico.* Albany: Institute for Mesoamerican Studies, State University of New York.

Kus, S. 1992: Toward an archaeology of body and soul. In J.-C. Gardin and C. S. Peebles (eds), *Representations in Archaeology,* Bloomington: Indiana University Press, 168–77.

Lamarque, P. 1990: Narrative and invention: The limits of fictionality. In C. Nash (ed.), *Narrative in Culture: The Uses of Storytelling in the Sciences, Philosophy, and Literature,* London: Routledge, 131–53.

Landau, M. 1991: *Narratives of Human Evolution: The Hero Story.* New Haven: Yale University Press.

Landow, G. 1992: *Hypertext: The Convergence of Contemporary Critical Theory and Technology.* Baltimore: Johns Hopkins University Press.

Latour, B. 1999: *Pandora's Hope: Essays on the Reality of Science Studies.* Cambridge, MA: Harvard University Press.

Lavine, S. D. 1991: Museum practices. In I. Karp and S. D. Lavine (eds), *Exhibiting Cultures: The Poetics and Politics of Museum Display,* Washington, DC: Smithsonian Institution Press, 151–8.

————1992: Audience, ownership, and authority: Designing relations between museums and communities. In I. Karp, C. M. Kreamer, and S. D. Lavine (eds), *Museums and Communities: The Politics of Public Culture,* Washington DC: Smithsonian Institution Press, 137–57.

Layton, R. 1989a: Introduction: Conflict in the archaeology of living traditions. In R. Layton (ed.), *Conflict in the Archaeology of Living Traditions,* London: Unwin Hyman, 1–21.

————(ed.) 1989b: *Who Needs the Past? Indigenous Values and Archaeology.* London: Unwin Hyman.

Leone, M. and Preucel, R. W. 1992: Archaeology in a democratic society. In L. Wandsnider (ed.), *Quandaries and Quests: Visions of Archaeology's Future,* Carbondale: Center for Archaeological Investigations, Southern Illinois University, 115–32.

Lesure, R. 1997: Figurines and social identities in early sedentary societies of coastal Chiapas, Mexico. In C. Claassen and R. A. Joyce (eds), *Women in Prehistory: North America and Mesoamerica,* Philadelphia: University of Pennsylvania Press, 227–48.

Levine, M. A. 1991: Historical overview of research on women in anthropology. In D. Walde and N. Willows (eds), *The Archaeology of Gender,* Proceedings of the 22nd Annual Chac Mool Conference, Calgary: Archaeological Association, University of Calgary, 177–86.

————1994: Creating their own niches: Career styles among women in Americanist archaeology between the wars. In C. Claassen (ed.), *Women in Archaeology,* Philadelphia: University of Pennsylvania Press, 9–40.

————1999: Uncovering a buried past: Women in Americanist archaeology before the First World War. In A. B. Kehoe and M. B. Emmerichs (eds), *Assembling the Past: Studies in the Professionalization of Archaeology*, Albuquerque: University of New Mexico Press, 133–51.

Lopez Austin, A. 1974: The research method of Fray Bernardino de Sahagún: The questionnaires. In M. Edmonson (ed.), *Sixteenth-Century Mexico: The Work of Sahagún*, Albuquerque: University of New Mexico Press, 111–50.

Lopiparo, J. 1994: Stones and bones at home: Reconstructing domestic activities from archaeological remains in a Terminal Classic residence, Ulúa Valley, Honduras. Senior honors thesis, Department of Anthropology, Harvard University, Cambridge, MA.

————2001: "Fractious Statelets" and "Galactic Polities": Ideology, ritual practices and the rise and fall of Classic Maya states. In C. Hastorf (ed.), *Archaeological Ritual*, Berkeley: Journal of the Kroeber Anthropological Society.

Lopiparo, J., Joyce, R. A., and Hendon, J. A. 2000: Terminal Classic pottery production in the Ulúa Valley, Honduras. Paper presented in the session "Terminal Classic Socioeconomic Processes in the Maya Lowlands Through a Ceramic Lens." Philadelphia: Society for American Archaeology.

Love, M. 1999: Ideology, material culture, and daily practice in Pre-Classic Mesoamerica: A Pacific Coast perspective. In D. C. Grove and R. A. Joyce (eds), *Social Patterns in Pre-Classic Mesamerica*, Washington, DC: Dumbarton Oaks Research Library and Collection, 127–53.

Lowenthal, D. 1990: Conclusion: Archaeologists and others. In P. Gathercole and D. Lowenthal (eds), *The Politics of the Past*, London: Unwin Hyman, 302–14.

Lynch, M. and Woolgar, S. (eds) 1990: *Representation in Scientific Practice*. Cambridge, MA: MIT Press.

Lynott, M. and Wylie, A. 1995: Stewardship: The central principle for archaeological ethics. In M. Lynott and A. Wylie (eds), *Ethics in American Archaeology: Challenges for the 1990s*, Washington, DC: Society for American Archaeology, 28–32.

Mandelker, A. (ed.) 1995: *Bakhtin in Contexts: Across the Disciplines*. Evanston, IL: Northwestern University Press.

Mannheim, B. and Tedlock, D. 1995: Introduction. In D. Tedlock and B. Mannheim (eds), *The Dialogic Emergence of Culture*, Urbana: University of Illinois Press, 1–32.

Marcus, G. E. and Fischer, M. M. J. 1986: *Anthropology as Cultural Critique: An Experimental Moment in the Human Sciences*. Chicago: University of Chicago Press.

McCafferty, S. and McCafferty, G. 1988: Powerful women and the myth of male dominance in Aztec society. *Archaeological Review from Cambridge* 7, 45–59.

———— 1991: Spinning and weaving as female gender identity in Post-Classic Mexico. In M. Schevill, J. C. Berlo, and E. Dwyer (eds), *Textile Traditions of Mesoamerica and the Andes: An Anthology*, New York: Garland, 19–44.

McDavid, C. 1999: From real space to cyberspace: Contemporary conversations about the archaeology of slavery and tenancy. *Internet Archaeology* 6 (http://intarch.ac.uk/journal/issue6/mcdavid/toc.html).

McDermott, R. P. and Tylbor, H. 1995: On the necessity of collusion in conversation. In D. Tedlock and B. Mannheim (eds), *The Dialogic Emergence of Culture*, Urbana: University of Illinois Press, 218–36.

McLuhan, M. 1994: *Understanding Media: The Extensions of Man*. Cambridge, MA: MIT Press.

Meskell, L. 1995: Goddesses, Gimbutas and "New Age" archaeology. *Antiquity* 69, 74–86.

———— 2000: Cycles of life and death: narrative homology and archaeological realities. *World Archaeology* 31, 423–41.

Mignolo, W. D. 1995: *The Darker Side of the Renaissance: Literacy, Territoriality, and Colonization*. Ann Arbor: University of Michigan Press.

Miller, D. 1998: Why some things matter. In D. Miller (ed.), *Material Cultures: Why Some Things Matter*, Chicago: University of Chicago Press, 3–21.

Molyneaux, B. (ed.) 1997: *The Cultural Life of Images: Visual Representation in Archaeology*. London: Routledge.

Moore, H. L. 1986: *Space, Text, and Gender: An Anthropological Study of the Marakwet of Kenya*. Cambridge: Cambridge University Press.

Morson, G. S. and Emerson, C. 1990: *Mikhail Bakhtin: Creation of a Prosaics*. Stanford: Stanford University Press.

Moser, S. 1992: Visions of the Australian Pleistocene: Prehistoric life at Lake Mungo and Kutikina. *Australian Archaeology* 35, 1–10.

———— 1996: Science, stratigraphy and the deep sequence: Excavation vs regional survey and the question of gendered practice in archaeology. *Antiquity* 70, 813–23.

———— 1998: *Ancestral Images: the Iconography of Human Origins*. Ithaca: Cornell University Press.

———— 1999: Gendered dimensions of archaeological practice: The stereotyping of archaeology as fieldwork. Revised version of a paper prepared for the SAR Advanced Seminar "Doing Archaeology as a Feminist." Margaret Conkey and Alison Wylie, organizers. Santa Fe, NM: School of American Research.

Mouer, L. D. 1998: Thomas Harris, Gent., as related by his second sonne. *Historical Archaeology* 32, 4–14.

Murphy, D., Beck, W., Brown, C., Perkins, T., Smith, A., and Somerville, M. 2000: *"No Man's Land": Camps at Corindi Lake South*. University of New England and Yarrawarra Aboriginal Corporation.

Murray, T. 1993: Introduction: The Sources of Archaeological Theory. In N. Yoffee and A. Sherratt (eds), *Archaeological Theory: Who Sets the Agenda?*, Cambridge: Cambridge University Press, 105–16.

Nash, J. 1978: The Aztecs and the ideology of male dominance. *Signs* 4, 349–62.

Nelson, M., Nelson, S., and Wylie, A. (eds) 1994: *Equity Issues for Women in Archeology*. Washington, DC: American Anthropological Association, Archeology Division, Archeology Papers Number 5.

Noel Hume, I. 1968: *Historical Archaeology*. New York: Alfred Knopf.

Norrick, N. R. 1997: Twice-told tales: Collaborative narration of familiar stories. *Language in Society* 26, 199–220.

Olsen, B. 1990: Roland Barthes: From sign to text. In C. Tilley (ed.), *Reading Material Culture: Structuralism, Hermeneutics and Post-Structuralism*, Oxford and Cambridge, MA: Basil Blackwell, 163–205.

Owoc, M. A. 1989: Reading, writing, and the resurrection of the subject. *Archaeological Review from Cambridge* 8, 165–74.

Pearson, M. P. and Richards, C. 1994: Ordering the world: Perceptions of architecture, space and time. In M. P. Pearson and C. Richards (eds), *Architecture and Order: Approaches to Social Space*, London: Routledge, 1–37.

Perin, C. 1992: The communicative circle: Museums as communities. In I. Karp, C. M. Kreamer, and S. D. Lavine (eds), *Museums and Communities: The Politics of Public Culture*, Washington DC: Smithsonian Institution Press, 182–220.

Petrie, W. M. F. 1904: *Methods and Aims in Archaeology*, New York: Macmillan.

Pluciennik, M. 1999: Archaeological narratives and other ways of telling. *Current Anthropology* 40, 653–78.

Praetzellis, A. 1998: Introduction: Why every archaeologist should tell stories once in a while. *Historical Archaeology* 32, 1:1–3.

——2000: *Death by Theory: A Tale of Mystery and Archaeological Theory*. Walnut Creek, CA: AltaMira Press.

Praetzellis, A. and Praetzellis, M. 1998: A Connecticut merchant in Chinadom: a play in one act. *Historical Archaeology* 32, 86–93.

Pred, A. 1984: Place as historically contingent process: Structuration and the time-geography of becoming places. *Annals of the Association of American Geographers* 74, 279–97.

——1990: *Making Histories and Constructing Human Geographies: The Local Transformation of Practice, Power Relations, and Consciousness*. Boulder: Westview Press.

Preucel, R. and Chesson, M. 1994: Blue Corn Girls: A Herstory of three early woman archaeologists at Tecolote, New Mexico. In C. Claassen (ed.), *Women in Archaeology*, Philadelphia: University of Pennsylvania Press, 67–84.

Price, D. W. 1999: *History Made, History Imagined: Contemporary Literature, Poiesis, and the Past*. Urbana: University of Illinois Press.

Propp, V. 1968: *Morphology of the Folktale*. Austin: University of Texas Press.

Rabinow, P. 1986: Representations are social facts: Modernity and postmodernity in anthropology. In J. Clifford and G. E. Marcus (eds), *Writing Culture: The Poetics and Politics of Ethnography*, Berkeley: University of California Press, 234–61.

Ray, R. B. 1995: *The Avant-Garde Finds Andy Hardy*. Cambridge, MA: Harvard University Press.

Renfrew, C. and Bahn, P. 1991: *Archaeology: Theories, Methods, and Practice*. London: Thames and Hudson.

Reyman, J. (ed.) 1992: *Rediscovering Our Past: Essays on the History of American Archaeology*. Aldershot: Avebury.

Rice, D. S. 1998: Classic to Postclassic Maya Household Transitions in Central Petén, Guatemala. In R. Wilk and W. Ashmore (eds), *Household and Community in the Mesoamerican Past*. Albuquerque: University of New Mexico Press, 227–47.

Rodman, M. C. 1992: Empowering place: Multilocality and multivocality. *American Anthropologist* 94, 640–56.

Rose, H. 1993: Rhetoric, feminism and scientific knowledge or from either/or to both/and. In R. H. Roberts and J. M. M. Good (eds), *The Recovery of Rhetoric: Persuasive Discourse and Disciplinarity in the Human Sciences*, Charlottesville: University Press of Virginia, 203–23.

Ryder, R. L. 1998: "Why I continue to live across the tracks from sister Sue," as told by William Monroe. *Historical Archaeology* 32, 34–41.

Sahagún, B. de 1950–82: [original ca. 1569] *Florentine Codex: The General History of the Things of New Spain*. C. E. Dibble and A. J. O. Anderson (trs and eds). Santa Fe, NM and Provo, UT: School of American Research and University of Utah Press.

—— 1993: [original ca. 1547] *Primeros Memoriales*. Facsimile edition, photographed by F. Anders. Norman: University of Oklahoma Press.

Sahlins, M. 1976: *Culture and Practical Reason*. Chicago: University of Chicago Press.

Salazar, P.-J. 1993: The unspeakable origin: Rhetoric and the social sciences, a reassessment of the French tradition. In R. H. Roberts and J. M. M. Good (eds), *The Recovery of Rhetoric: Persuasive Discourse and Disciplinarity in the Human Sciences*, Charlottesville: University Press of Virginia, 101–16.

Schmidt, P. R. and Patterson, T. C. (eds) 1995: *Making Alternative Histories: The Practice of Archaeology and History in Non-Western Settings*. Santa Fe, NM: School of American Research Press.

Serra, M. C. and Sugiura, Y. 1987: Funerary rites at two historical moments in Mesoamerica: Middle and Late Formative. In L. Manzanilla (ed.), *Studies in the Neolithic and Urban Revolutions: The V. Gordon Childe Colloquium, Mexico, 1986*, Oxford: BAR International Series 349, 345–51.

Shanks, M. 1992: *Experiencing the Past*. London: Routledge.

———1995: Archaeology and the forms of history. In I. Hodder, M. Shanks, A. Alexandri, V. Buchli, J. Carman, J. Last, and G. Lucas (eds), *Interpreting Archaeology: Finding Meaning in the Past*, London: Routledge, 169–74.

———1997: Photography and archaeology. In B. Molyneaux (ed.), *The Cultural Life of Images: Visual Representation in Archaeology*, London: Routledge, 73–107.

Shanks, M. and Hodder, I. 1995: Introduction. In I. Hodder, M. Shanks, A. Alexandri, V. Buchli, J. Carman, J. Last, and G. Lucas (eds), *Interpreting Archaeology: Finding Meaning in the Past*, London: Routledge, 3–29.

Shanks, M. and Tilley, C. 1987: *Re-Constructing Archaeology: Theory and Practice*. Cambridge: Cambridge University Press.

Sheets, P. 1992: The pervasive pejorative in Intermediate Area Studies. In F. W. Lange (ed.), *Wealth and Hierarchy in the Intermediate Area*, Washington, DC: Dumbarton Oaks Research Library and Collection, 15–42.

Sinclair, A. 1989: This is an article about archaeology as writing. *Archaeological Review from Cambridge* 8, 212–31.

Smith, B. C. 1994: A case study of applied feminist theories. In J. R. Glaser and A. A. Zenetou (eds), *Gender Perspectives: Essays on Women in Museums*, Washington, DC: Smithsonian Institution Press, 137–46.

Somerville, M., Beck, W., Brown, C., Murphy, D., Perkins, T., and Smith, A. 1999: *Arrawarra: Meeting Place*, University of New England and Yarrawarra Aboriginal Corporation.

Spector, J. 1991: What this awl means: Toward a feminist archaeology. In J. Gero and M. Conkey (eds), *Engendering Archaeology: Women and Prehistory*, Oxford: Basil Blackwell, 388–406.

———1993: *What this Awl Means: Feminist Archaeology at a Wahpeton Dakota Village*. St. Paul: Minnesota Historical Society Press.

Sperber, D. 1992: Culture and matter. In J.-C. Gardin and C. S. Peebles (eds), *Representations in Archaeology*, Bloomington: Indiana University Press, 56–65.

Sterud, E. L. 1978: Changing aims of Americanist archaeology: A citations analysis of American Antiquity 1946–1975. *American Antiquity* 43, 294–302.

Stevanovic, M. 1997: The age of clay: The social dynamics of house destruction. *Journal of Anthropological Archaeology* 16, 334–95.

———2000: Visualizing and vocalizing the archaeological *archival* record: Narrative vs image. In I. Hodder (ed.), *Towards a Reflexive Method in Archaeology: The Example at Çatalhöyük*, British Institute of Archaeology at Ankara Monograph No. 28, Cambridge: McDonald Institute for Archaeological Research, 235–8.

Stevens, C. 1997: "Is academic archaeological writing boring?" "Maybe"; "Uninteresting?" "Never": a reply to Boivin. *Archaeological Review from Cambridge* 14, 127–40.

Tannen, D. 1995: Waiting for the mouse: Constructed dialogue in conversation. In D. Tedlock and B. Mannheim (eds), *The Dialogic Emergence of
Culture*, Urbana: University of Illinois Press, 198–217.

Taylor, W. W. 1948: *A Study of Archaeology*. Washington, DC: American
Anthropological Association, Memoir Number 69.

Tchen, J. K. W. 1992: Creating a dialogic museum: The Chinatown History
Museum experiment. In I. Karp, C. M. Kreamer, and S. D. Lavine (eds),
Museums and Communities: The Politics of Public Culture, Washington
DC: Smithsonian Institution Press, 285–326.

Tedlock, D. 1993: *Breath on the Mirror: Mythic Voices and Visions of the
Lining Maya*. San Francisco: HarperSanFrancisco.

———1995: Interpretation, participation, and the role of narrative in dialogical anthropology. In D. Tedlock and B. Mannheim (eds), *The Dialogic
Emergence of Culture*, Urbana: University of Illinois Press, 253–87.

Terrell, J. 1990: Storytelling and prehistory. *Archaeological Method and
Theory* 2, 1–29.

Thomas, J. 1990: Same, other, analogue: writing the past. In F. Baker, S.
Taylor, and J. Thomas (eds), *Writing the Past in the Present*, Lampeter: St.
David's University College, 18–23.

Thompson, R. H. 1956: The subjective element in archaeological inference.
Southwestern Journal of Anthropology 12, 327–32.

Tilley, C. 1989 1993a: Interpretation and a poetics of the past. In C. Tilley
(ed.), *Interpretive Archaeology*, Providence and Oxford: Berg, 1–27.

———1993b: Prospecting Archaeology. In C. Tilley (ed.), *Interpretive
Archaeology*, Providence and Oxford: Berg, 395–416.

———1999: *Metaphor and Material Culture*. Oxford: Blackwell.

Todorov, T. 1984: *Mikhail Bakhtin: The Dialogical Principle*. Wlad Godzich
(tr.). Minneapolis: University of Minnesota Press.

Tolstoy, P. 1989: Coapexco and Tlatilco: Sites with Olmec materials in the
Basin of Mexico. In R. J. Sharer and D. C. Grove (eds), *Regional Perspectives on the Olmec*, Cambridge: Cambridge University Press, 85–121.

Trawick, M. 1988: Spirits and voices in Tamil songs. *American Ethnologist*
15, 193–215.

Trigger, B. G. 1989: *A History of Archaeological Thought*. Cambridge:
Cambridge University Press.

Tringham, R. E. 1991: Households with faces: The challenge of gender in
prehistoric architectural remains. In J. Gero and M. Conkey (eds), *Engendering Archaeology: Women and Prehistory*, Oxford: Basil Blackwell,
93–131.

———1994: Engendered places in prehistory. *Gender, Place, and Culture* 1,
169–203.

———1995: Archaeological houses, households, housework and the home.
In D. Benjamin and D. Stea (eds), *The Home: Words, Interpretations,
Meanings, and Environments*, Aldershot: Avebury Press, 79–107.

———1996: But Gordon, where are the people? Some comments on
the topic of craft specialization and social evolution. In B. Wailes (ed.),

Craft Specialization and Social Evolution: In commemoration of V. Gordon Childe, Philadelphia: MASCA Press, University of Pennsylvania, 233–9.

———1998: Multimedia authoring and the feminist practice of archaeology. Paper prepared for the SAR Advanced Seminar "Doing Archaeology as a Feminist." Margaret Conkey and Alison Wylie, organizers. Santa Fe, NM: School of American Research.

———2000: The continuous house: A view from the deep past. In R. A. Joyce and S. D. Gillespie (eds), *Beyond Kinship: Social and Material Reproduction in House Societies*, Philadelphia: University of Pennsylvania Press, 115–34.

Tufte, E. R. 1983: *The Visual Display of Quantitative Information*. Cheshire, CT: Graphics Press.

———1990: *Envisioning Information*. Cheshire, CT: Graphics Press.

Urban, P. A. and Smith, S. 1987: The incensarios and candeleros of central Santa Bárbara: Distributional and functional studies. In E. J. Robinson (ed.), *Interaction on the Southeast Mesoamerican Frontier: Prehistoric and Historic Honduras and El Salvador*. Oxford: BAR International Series 327.

Victor, K. L. and Beaudry, M. C. 1992: Women's participation in American prehistoric and historical archaeology: A comparative look at the journals *American Antiquity* and *Historical Archaeology*. In C. Claassen (ed.), *Exploring Gender Through Archaeology: Selected Papers from the 1991 Boone Conference*, Monographs in World Archaeology, No. 11, Madison, WI: Prehistory Press, 11–21.

Visweswaran, K. 1994: *Fictions of Feminist Ethnography*. Minneapolis: University of Minnesota Press.

———1997: Histories of feminist ethnography. *Annual Reviews in Anthropology* 26, 591–621.

Weiner, A. 1992: *Inalienable Possessions: The Paradox of Keeping-While-Giving*. Berkeley: University of California Press.

Weiss, W. A. 1990: Challenge to authority: Bakhtin and ethnographic description. *Cultural Anthropology* 5, 414–30.

White, H. 1973: *Metahistory: The Historical Imagination in Nineteenth Century Europe*. Baltimore: Johns Hopkins University Press.

———1978: *Tropics of Discourse: Essays in Cultural Criticism*. Baltimore: Johns Hopkins University Press.

———1987: *The Content of the Form: Narrative Discourse and Historical Representation*. Baltimore: Johns Hopkins University Press.

Wolf, M. 1992: *A Thrice Told Tale: Feminism, Postmodernism, and Ethnographic Responsibility*. Stanford: Stanford University Press.

Wolle, A.-C. and Tringham, R. E. 2000: Multiple Çatalhöyüks on the World Wide Web. In I. Hodder (ed.), *Towards a Reflexive Method in Archaeology: The Example at Çatalhöyük*, British Institute of Archaeology at Ankara Monograph No. 28, Cambridge: McDonald Institute for Archaeological Research, 207–17.

Wylie, A. 1989: Archaeological cables and tacking: The implications of practice for Bernstein's "Options beyond objectivism and relativism." *Philosophy of the Social Sciences* 19, 1–18.

———1992a: The interplay of evidential constraints and political interests: Recent archaeological research on gender. *American Antiquity* 57, 15–35.

———1992b: Rethinking the Quincentennial: Consequences for past and present. *American Antiquity* 57, 591–4.

———1995: Alternative histories: Epistemic disunity and political integrity. In P. R. Schmidt and T. C. Patterson (eds), *Making Alternative Histories: The Practice of Archaeology and History in Non-Western Settings*, Santa Fe, NM: School of American Research Press, 255–72.

———1996: Ethical dilemmas in archaeological practice: Looting, repatriation, stewardship, and the (trans)formation of disciplinary identity. *Perspectives on Science* 4, 154–194.

———In press: *Thinking From Things: Essays in the Philosophy of Archaeology*. Berkeley: University of California Press.

Yamin, R. 1998: Lurid tales and homely stories of New York's notorious Five Points. *Historical Archaeology* 32, 74–85.

Yellen, J. 1983: Women, archaeology, and the National Science Foundation. In J. Gero, D. Lacy, and M. Blakey (eds), *The Socio-Politics of Archaeology*, Department of Anthropology, Research Report No. 23, Amherst, MA: Department of Anthropology, University of Massachusetts, 59–65.

———1991: Women, archaeology, and the National Science Foundation: An analysis of fiscal year 1989 data. In D. Walde and N. Willows (eds), *The Archaeology of Gender*, Proceedings of the 22nd Annual Chac Mool Conference, Calgary: Archaeological Association, University of Calgary, 201–10.

Yoffee, N. and Sherratt, A. 1993: Introduction: The sources of archaeological theory. In N. Yoffee and A. Sherratt (eds), *Archaeological Theory: Who Sets the Agenda?*, Cambridge: Cambridge University Press, 1–9.

Zeder, M. 1997: *The American Archaeologist: A Profile*. Walnut Creek, CA: AltaMira Press.

Index

ceramics, *see* pottery
Cerro Palenque 41, 43, 81
Chesson, Meredith 19, 21
chronotope (time–space) 51–2, 59,
  61, 75, 143; of adventure time 35;
  of archaeological reports 138; of
  discovery 34–5, 52; of
  eschatology 35–6; of evolution
  34–5; of experience 34–5; of
  progress 34–5; in work of
  Mikhail Bakhtin 34–5
citation 32–3, 59, 63, 127, 141
Clifford, James 55
closure, *see* unfinalizability
collaboration 3, 6, 23, 56, 101–3,
  117–20, 130
communication 16, 67, 113, 119; in
  work of Mikhail Bakhtin 9–10,
  29–32, 61, 142; in work of Jürgen
  Habermas, 31
conceptual archive 47–8
Conkey, Margaret 19, 27
context 10, 16, 127; total, of
  communication 29–32, 61
Copan 42–3, 47
Costello, Julia 66–7
cowboy, as metaphor for
  archaeologist 27
craft production 81–2, 84–5, 87; as
  metaphor for archaeology 81, 85
cultivation, as metaphor for
  archaeology 24–5, 85

De Cunzo, Lu Ann 122
Deetz, James 6, 54, 121
determinism 14
dialogue, in archaeology 2–3, 5–6,
  28–9, 56, 58, 127, 134; in
  archaeological writing 56–67,
  103, 119, 124; constructed from
  quotes 59–67, 87, 122–3; with
  fictional characters 56–9; in
  museum exhibit planning 130;
  outside discipline of archaeology
  29, 67, 115, 126–9, 129–31;

relation to narrative 12–14, 54,
  100; in work of Mikhail Bakhtin
  7–10, 29–31, 76
difference 5, 11, 115, 123, 132, 139,
  143
discourse, narrative discriminated
  from 12
discovery, as chronotope 34–5, 52
double-voicedness 46, 53, 119;
  defined 8–9
dualism subject-object 16–17

emotion 57–8, 116, 145
empirical adequacy 121
eschatology, as chronotope 35–6
ethics, in archaeology 74–5, 101; in
  hypertext theory 77; in work of
  Mikhail Bakhtin 8, 14, 16, 76
ethnography, authority 55; feminist
  3; genres 55–6; polyphony 55–6;
  postmodern 3
evaluation, *see* answerability
Evasdottir, Erika 21
evolution, as chronotope 34–5
exhibits, *see* museum
experience 58, 74, 116; archaeology
  as 23–4; as chronotope 34–5; and
  skill 26, 114

Fabian, Johannes 125–6
features 5, 40, 65
feminist research 3, 18–21, 28, 32,
  65, 74, 119–20
field schools 19
fieldwork 5–6, 18–19; collaborative
  23; gendered male 19–22;
  identified with excavation 19;
  metaphors 21–2; narratives
  24–6, 47; products of 23
finalization 67, 80; provisional
  15–16, 133–4
Flannery, Kent 56, 129
Florentine Codex 101, 103, 118
formalism 36–7; critiques of 9, 13,
  135

Galloway, Patricia 118
Gardin, Jean-Claude 137
Gass, William 122
gender 19–22, 104–10, 119, 124,
139, 141, 145–50; *see also* feminist
research
Gennette, Gérard 13
genres, in archaeology 2, 5–6, 33,
50–1, 129–30, 135; in
ethnography 55–6; in history 14;
in work of Mikhail Bakhtin 34,
36–8, 100
Gero, Joan 19, 27
gestures 10, 122, 134
Giddens, Anthony 116
Gillespie, Susan 83
Goddess Movement 29
graphics, in archaeological texts 2,
15–16, 128, 135–7, 139; dialogic
137; in fieldwork 5, 41; in
hypermedia 88; in museum
exhibits 130–1
Guyer, Carolyn 101, 115, 120–1

habitus 69, 76
Haraway, Donna 19–21, 119
Harding, Sandra 74, 119–20
Harré, Rom 53–4
hermeneutics 30
Hero Quest 23, 27
Herzfeld, Michael 134
Hesse, Mary 25
heteroglossia 16, 37, 61, 65; in
archaeology 10, 26–8, 47, 50,
127, 135, 143; defined 10–11, 79
Hodder, Ian 1, 36, 52, 129, 133
Holquist, Michael 7
Honduras, archaeology in 5–6,
39–45, 50–1, 81–8
household archaeology 34, 46, 69,
73–4, 81–4, 86, 139–40
human sciences, in work of Mikhail
Bakhtin 8, 10, 75, 100, 123
hypermedia 69; construction of
77–8, 83–8; dangers of 121;

metaphors in 83–6; and
multivocality 76–7, 103, 120–1;
navigation of 83–6; as writerly
medium 78–81
hypertext 60, 77–9, 101, 119;
dialogic construction of 111–13;
knowledge construction in 115,
117; links 87–8

incensario 41–4, 47–8, 87
Indiana Jones 27, 35
inscription, practices of 70
intentionality 71–2, 142

Johnson, Matthew 56, 129
journals 64–5
Joyce, Michael 101, 119, 129
Joyce, Rosemary 63, 74–5

Kelly, Isabel 19
knowledge construction 115, 120;
archaeological 1, 7, 25, 69, 113,
138; through dialogue 7–8, 47,
52, 54, 66, 123; in museum
exhibits 130–1

language, dialogic concept of 7–8;
as relation between three parties
8–9; stratification of 10–12,
27–9
Lara Croft 28
Latin American Antiquity 50–1
Latour, Bruno 136–7
letters 52–3, 55
loma 40–2, 45, 47, 49–50; *see also*
tell
Lopiparo, Jeanne 39, 132

Mantecales 39–46, 48–9, 52, 55
material culture 70–3, 75–6, 80–1,
83, 87; as evidence 136; as
utterance 52, 66, 69–70, 82, 84,
100–1, 117, 126, 141–3
Maya, Classic 42, 46, 48, 63, 81–2,
84